WEEKENDS FOR TWO IN THE WINE COUNTRY

BILL GLEESON | PHOTOGRAPHS BY RICHARD GILLETTE

weekends for two

IN THE
WINE COUNTRY

50 ROMANTIC NORTHERN CALIFORNIA GETAWAYS

CHRONICLE BOOKS

SAN FRANCISCO

Text copyright © 2003 by Bill Gleeson.

Photographs copyright © 2003 by Richard Gillette.

Library of Congress Cataloging-in-Publication
Data available.

ISBN 0-8118-3527-8

Manufactured in China.

Designed and typeset by Deborah Bowman.

The author wishes to thank Yvonne Gleeson.

Distributed in Canada by Raincoast Books
9050 Shaughnessy Street
Vancouver, British Columbia V6P 6E5

10 9 8 7 6 5 4 3 2 1

Chronicle Books LLC
85 Second Street
San Francisco, California 94105

www.chroniclebooks.com

Front cover: Kenwood Inn, Kenwood, page 50.

Table of Contents

A stroll through an enchanting Italian-style villa, a slow drive through vineyard-covered hills, the lustrous garnet of a Cabernet against the light of a flickering fire. There are few things more romantic than wine and wine making.

Since my wife, Yvonne, and I began our romantic wanderings more than a decade ago in search of destinations worthy of *Weekends for Two* status, Northern California's wine-making regions have continued to blossom and mature. California vintages rank with—and often outrank—those produced in Europe. World-class culinary artistry has followed and flourished. And despite tourism and development, the natural beauty of these regions endures.

For those whose passions are stirred by fine wine, food, and nature, there's nothing more romantic than a visit to the source. And in Northern California, traveling romantics have an ever-growing number of options.

Through a happy coincidence, a number of new inns, small hotels, and restaurants began welcoming visitors in various wine-making regions during the course of our travels associated with this particular volume. Many existing inns also emerged anew from extensive makeovers, while famous chefs branched out and broadened their mastery with new dinner houses, bistros, and grills.

Mindful that wine making and winery touring have pushed the traditional boundaries of Napa, Sonoma, and Mendocino Counties, we've also included destinations in a few other romantic regions that are worthy of a romantic weekend wine-country getaway.

ROOMS FOR ROMANCE

Our goal in creating this and the many other books in the *Weekends for Two* series is to take the mystery and guesswork out of choosing a destination for a special romantic getaway. During the course of our travels, we've toured hundreds of inns and literally thousands of guest rooms in an effort to bring some definition to that often-maligned term, *romantic*.

Our journeys have taken us from the coast of Maine to California's Catalina Island, and from the Canadian Gulf Islands to the sleepy towns of New Mexico. We've slept in countless guest rooms and received input from hundreds of readers. Following are some of the features we like.

- Private bathrooms; a must in our opinion. We'll tell you if any are shared or detached.
- In-room fireplaces.
- Tubs and showers big enough for two; because a bathroom can be a romantic destination unto itself.
- Breakfast in bed; many traveling romantics don't fancy sharing a communal table with strangers.
- Feather beds and cushy comforters; need we say more?
- Comfortable couches, chaises, or love seats; the bed shouldn't be the only piece of furniture where two can be together.

- Lamps, sconces, and candles; overhead lighting isn't particularly romantic.
- Private decks, patios, or balconies; most of us enjoy the inspiration of the outdoors.
- Rooms where smoking is never permitted.

Although few, if any, of our chosen destinations offer this complete list of romantic ingredients, each offers at least some of these features. And we endeavor to point them out, along with the occasional critical caveat concerning noise, bathroom size, location, furnishings, and so on.

THE PRICE OF ROMANCE

If a special occasion is worthy of a special bottle of wine or meal, it also deserves a memorable place to stay and play. Accordingly, you should be prepared to invest a little more for a romantic room fit for a special occasion.

To help you plan your getaway budget, approximate 2003 rates are included for many of the rooms we describe. These rates are always subject to change. If you're booking a weekend trip, please also note that many establishments require two-night minimum stays. Some holidays command three-night minimums. Harvest season (fall months) attracts the most visitors, so book early.

Rates (per high-season weekend night for two friendly people) are classified at the end of each listing using the following ranges, not including tax:

Moderate: Under $200
Expensive: $200 – $300
Deluxe: Over $300

FINAL NOTES

No payment was sought or accepted from any establishment in exchange for being included in this book. We make the decisions about which properties to include and how they're described.

Please understand that we cannot guarantee that these properties will maintain furnishings or standards as they existed at the time of our visit. We very much appreciate hearing from readers if their experience is at variance with our descriptions. Reader comments will be carefully consulted for future revisions of this book. Please send comments, suggestions, and ideas to Bill Gleeson in care of Chronicle Books at the address listed on the copyright page.

Food, wine, and flowers may have been added to some rooms for photograph styling purposes. Some inns provide such amenities; others do not. Please ask when making a reservation whether these items are complimentary or whether they're provided for an extra charge.

BASICS OF WINE TASTING

Wine makers and tasting-bar hosts have their own unique methods for tasting, and they're typically happy to pass along their techniques to visitors. You'll generally start with dry white wines, moving next to sweet whites, and finishing with reds.

Some years ago, during a visit to charming Buena Vista Winery in Sonoma, we were greeted with printed no-nonsense instructions in the art of wine tasting, revised here. At Buena Vista, this was called the "S" method of tasting.

- SEE

   Hold your glass at eye level and take note of the wine's color and clarity. The wine shouldn't appear cloudy or dull (sediment is ok). Red wines become lighter as they age, while white wines darken.

- SWIRL

   Gently swirl the glass, releasing the wine's aroma and bouquet. *Aroma* is the smell of the grape in the wine; *bouquet* refers to the scents that result from aging and fermentation.

- SNIFF

   Bring the glass close to your nose and inhale deeply. Try to pick out the different scents. Smelling a wine is important, since most of what you think is taste is in fact linked to smell. Most of the time you'll be greeted by pleasant aromas, but olfactory warning signs include a burning-match smell (too much sulfur dioxide preservative) or a sour smell (too much acetic acid).

- SIP

   Take a sip of the wine and swirl it around in your mouth, making sure it encounters your whole tongue, so you'll be able to pick up all the subtle tastes. You'll notice definite flavors and sensations. For example, you might be able to detect the flavor of fruits like pear and apple in a Chardonnay. A Merlot or Cabernet may yield flavors of currant, cherry, or plum. Try to describe the wine's *body,* or mouth feel. Is it light, medium, or full-bodied?

- SAVOR

   After you swallow, take a moment to savor the lingering tastes and sensations in your mouth. This impression is referred to as the wine's *finish.*

DISCOVERING BACKROAD WINERIES

After you've fought with the tourists for a smidgen of space at one of those large winery tasting bars, and after you've been herded, sheeplike, through long, anonymous winery tours, it's time to follow the lead of poet Robert Frost and take "the road less traveled by."

Many of the large wineries, with their well-stocked kitchen-and-wine shops, are definitely worth a visit. That being said, we strongly encourage wine-country travelers to venture off Napa Valley's Highway 29 or Sonoma County's Highway 101 for a chance to experience the wine industry in an unhurried, Old World, informal way. At many small wine-making operations, tastings and tours are led by owners and family members who play personal roles in producing their wines.

Unless you're a veteran of the California back-country wine roads, chances are you'll be unfamiliar with many of the smaller wineries you'll pass by on the way to a country inn or during an afternoon of off-the-beaten-track tasting.

Because of their comparatively small size and output, many Northern California wineries—especially those along the back roads—lack the retail clout and restaurant distribution channels that the large wine-making operations enjoy. In fact, many small wineries sell just about all their wines through their tasting rooms.

MAKING AN APPOINTMENT

A few small wineries are open to the public by appointment only. To many, making an appointment to taste wine may sound somewhat off-putting, especially when there are so many wineries that are open all day, every day. Keep in mind that wine makers don't request appointments out of arrogance. These folks spend a good part of their day tending wines and vines. So if you drop by unannounced, you may find the owners in the lab, pruning vines, irrigating fields, or bottling wine. For most vintners who request a call in advance, twenty-four hours' notice is generally sufficient. Better yet, ask your innkeeper to recommend one of his or her favorite small wineries and make a reservation for you. And don't forget to acknowledge the proprietor's time by purchasing a bottle or two.

RESPONSIBLE TOURING

Wine touring can be one of the most pleasant ways to spend a day or a weekend. Don't spoil your day (or someone else's) by overindulging at the tasting bar or picnic table.

According to the California Highway Patrol, drinking more than eight ounces of wine over a two-hour period could put you into the "driving under the influence" category. Remember, those wine samples add up quickly.

Many wineries serve complimentary coffee, soda, or grape juice to designated drivers. There are also chauffeured limousines and vintage cars that will squire you to and from the wineries of your choice. Ask your innkeeper to help with arrangements. We encourage everyone to do their part to keep the wine-country roads safe.

GRAPE ESCAPES

Leave the crowds behind and venture west up Redwood Road off Highway 29 in NAPA. Among the foothills and forests you'll find Hess Collection Winery, which pairs the art of wine making with the owner's powerful collection of contemporary art.

Not far away, at the top of a hill in the CARNEROS REGION between Highways 12 and 29, is the stunning Artesa Vineyards and Winery. On a clear day you can see San Francisco. There's a small museum here, as well as a relaxing tasting area and outside seating.

At the north end of the valley, the storybook-style medieval facade and lush Chinese gardens of CALISTOGA's Chatêau Montelena are a must-see.

TABLES FOR TWO

You may purchase gourmet picnic fixings at the famous Oakville Grocery on Highway 29 in OAKVILLE, or at Dean & Deluca in ST. HELENA. Tra Vigne restaurant in St. Helena has an on-site takeout deli that features tasty sandwiches and salads. There are a number of picnic tables at V. Sattui Winery between St. Helena and Rutherford. Vichon Winery, on Oakville Grade Road just west of Highway 29, has an oak-shaded picnic area with romantic vineyard, valley, and mountain views. Etiquette note: If you picnic at a winery, it's bad form—and may even be against the winery's rules—to drink wine brought in from another establishment.

In NAPA, our innkeepers recommend Tuscany, Celadon, and Coles Chop House. A longtime personal favorite just north of Napa on Highway 29 is Mustards Grill. In ST. HELENA, we recommend Tra Vigne, Pinot Blanc, and Pat Kuleto's new Martini House. In CALISTOGA, our picks include Wappo Bar and Bistro, Calistoga Inn, and Catahoula.

Finally, be advised that dinner at the world-famous French Laundry in YOUNTVILLE isn't a last-minute decision. You should call months in advance (707-944-2380).

THE NAPA VALLEY

NAPA RIVER INN
500 Main Street
Napa, CA 94559
Telephone: (707) 251-8500;
toll-free: (877) 251-8500
Web site: www.napariverinn.com

THE FACTS

Sixty-six rooms, each with private bath; more than half with gas fireplaces, eight with oversized soaking tubs. Complimentary full breakfast served in inn's bakery or delivered to your room. Complimentary cocktails served in evening. Complimentary newspaper. Twice-daily maid service. Restaurant, day spa, and local van service. Two-night minimum stay required during weekends, three-night minimum during holiday periods. Disabled access. Expensive to deluxe.

GETTING THERE

From Highway 29 in Napa, exit east at First Street and follow signs to downtown Napa. Turn right on California Boulevard and left on Second Street (one way). Follow Second Street to Main Street. Turn right on Main Street and follow to inn at the corner of Main and Fifth Streets.

NAPA RIVER INN

The bustling downtown district of Napa, long a bastion of quaint Victorian bed-and-breakfast inns, has undergone a renaissance of sorts in recent years. Downtown Napa has seen a surge of fine restaurant openings and development projects, including the American Center for Wine, Food and the Arts (known as COPIA) and the restoration of the historic Napa Valley Opera House.

Napa River Inn, a luxury boutique hotel anchoring the historic Napa Mill Project along the Napa River, is also among the new arrivals. Home to a growing number of shops, markets, and restaurants, the mill project represents the largest historic-redevelopment undertaking in the history of the wine-country capital.

ROOMS FOR ROMANCE

You'll need to make multiple visits to sample the varied accommodations at Napa River Inn. A handful of historic deluxe rooms (around $400) in the inn's main Hatt Building reflect the history of the mill property. These have maple-wood floors, exposed-brick walls, sitting areas with fireplaces, partially canopied beds, comfy lounge chairs and ottomans, and historic regional art. The bathrooms are equipped with old-style "slipper" tubs and separate showers.

A nautical theme is evident in the Embarcadero Building's twenty-six cheery yellow rooms. Accommodations here offer Napa River views along with brass fittings and cherry wood paneled walls and wainscoting, as well as fireplaces and private balconies.

About half of the inn's sixty-six rooms are located in what is called the Plaza Building. These feature a more rustic décor, with handsome oak furniture and art reminiscent of old California. The bathrooms are white marble.

Napa River Inn is perfectly situated for downtown Napa explorations, and is a short stroll away from attractions such as the Wine Train as well as COPIA, which offers a changing schedule of cooking- and wine-related workshops and activities.

THE FACTS

Seven rooms, each with private bath. Complimentary full breakfast served at tables for two (Buckley House) or more (in the main inn). Complimentary wine and refreshments served in evening. Complimentary beverages and fruit available at all times. No disabled access. Two- or three-night minimum stay required during weekends and holiday periods. Moderate to expensive.

GETTING THERE

From Highway 29 in Napa, exit east at First Street and follow signs to downtown Napa. Turn right on California Boulevard and left on Second Street (one way). Follow Second Street (one way) for approximately four blocks to first traffic light (Jefferson Street) and turn left. Drive four blocks to Calistoga Avenue and turn right. Follow to inn on corner of Seminary Street and Calistoga Avenue.

LA BELLE EPOQUE
1386 Calistoga Avenue
Napa, CA 94559
Telephone: (707) 257-2161;
toll-free: (800) 238-8070
Web site: labelleepoque.com

LA BELLE EPOQUE

Choosing the perfect getaway destination from among Napa Valley's myriad hotels and bed-and-breakfast inns can be a challenging task, especially in the eclectic Napa area. And because they've not all been, shall we say, created equal, making the wrong choice can have disappointing consequences. In fact, the idea for the *Weekends for Two* series was born after we made a particularly poor pick right here in Napa.

In the years since, we've done plenty of exploring, and along with some unmentionables, we've discovered some absolute gems. Among them is La Belle Epoque, which blends Napa's charming Victorian past with just the right level of contemporary comforts.

The setting is a stunning landmark Victorian with a raised front porch and lots of stained glass, gables, and gingerbread. It's part of the historic Old Town residential area, which is just a short stroll away from the downtown district. Those who like to stay connected to the real world will appreciate the in-room data ports, voice mail, cable TVs, videocassette players, and compact disc players.

ROOMS FOR ROMANCE

A most decadent wine-country retreat is the Champagne Suite (around $300). Located on the ground floor, the suite has an elevated king-sized bed, a dressing room, and a sitting area. The bathroom has a spa tub for two. What's more, the occupants of this room have exclusive use (after 8 P.M.) of the inn's wine-tasting room, which has a fireplace, a wet bar, and an entertainment center.

The centerpiece of Cabernet (mid $200 range) is a gorgeous elevated king-sized bed with a net canopy. The bathroom has a shower for two.

Gamay (mid $200 range) is the epitome of romance. In addition to a queen-sized carved Victorian bed under an ornate ceiling treatment, the room has a stained-glass-windowed sitting area furnished with a love seat. You'll also be treated to a spa tub for two with shower.

Set under the second-floor eaves, Chardonnay (mid $200 range) features lots of stained glass and has a queen-sized bed and a sitting area with a fireplace. The bathroom has a shower for two.

A charming garden-view sitting area is among the romantic attributes of Merlot (mid $200 range), whose king-sized brass bed has a wall canopy. The bathroom has a spa tub for one.

Not long ago, innkeeper Georgia Jump acquired the Buckley House, another historic Victorian just across the street. Two luxury suites are available here. Elizabeth's Suite (low $300 range) is decorated in French country blue-and-white toile. It has a fireplace and a love seat, as well as a refrigerator and a microwave. The bathroom has a stained-glass window and a spa tub for two.

Caroline's Suite (low $300 range) has a separate living room with a love seat and an antique buffet that houses a microwave and a refrigerator. The bedroom features a wall-canopied raised king-sized bed, an antique love seat, and a French armoire.

THE FACTS

Ten rooms, each with private bath. Complimentary full breakfast served in main inn and delivered to each cottage unit. Complimentary refreshments served in afternoon. Disabled access. Two-night minimum stay required during weekends. Moderate to expensive.

GETTING THERE

From Highway 29 in Napa, exit east at First Street and follow signs to downtown Napa. Turn right on California Boulevard and left on Second Street (one way). Follow Second Street to Randolph Street. Turn right on Randolph and follow to inn.

INN ON RANDOLPH
411 Randolph Street
Napa, CA 94559
Telephone: (707) 257-2886;
toll-free: (800) 670-6886
Web site: www.innonrandolph.com

Passersby who might be tempted to label Inn on Randolph as just another lovely Victorian-era home-turned-inn will do well to remember the adage: "Don't judge a book by its cover." Unlike many grand Napa bed-and-breakfast inns that are squeezed tightly on smallish parcels, Inn on Randolph occupies a half-acre of landscaped grounds and offers some hidden romantic accommodations that we typically find only at country properties.

ROOMS FOR ROMANCE

Dating from 1860, the main inn is one of Napa's oldest Victorians, a wonderfully restored example of the Gothic Revival style. There are five comfortable rooms here, and two of them—called Winter and Autumn—have spa tubs for two. Rates for these two rooms are around $200.

What truly sets Inn on Randolph apart from other in-town inns are the three 1930s-era cottages that share the spacious grounds. Each cottage unit offers a television, a compact disc player, a videocassette player, a refrigerator, and a coffeemaker. Breakfast is delivered to your door.

Arguably the most romantic is the private Arbor Cottage (around $300), a spacious bungalow nicely decorated in terra-cotta and sage green tones. The furnishings include a pretty, queen-sized pine bed and a cushy love seat, both of which face a fireplace. There's also a kitchenette with a refrigerator, a microwave, and a coffeemaker. The bathroom has both a two-person shower and a spa tub for two. The cottage also features a namesake arbor and a stone patio.

Laurel Cottage consists of the Lodge and Terrace rooms (upper $200 range). Set behind a picket fence, the Lodge, with its eclectic mix of woods, deep green hues, and river-rock fireplace, might bring to mind a grand hunting lodge. This very cozy retreat has a king-sized pine and iron bed and a distressed-pine armoire in which sit a television, a videocassette player, and a compact disc player. The impressive floor-to-ceiling rock-walled fireplace stands in the adjoining dining nook. There's a tub for two and a shower in the bathroom.

Next door, the Terrace (upper $200 range) offers more of a garden-cottage theme. It has a private brick terrace where guests might enjoy breakfast on a nice morning. Inside is a queen-sized bed and a fireplace. The bathroom has a spa tub for two and a shower.

Randolph Cottage also has two rooms: the Library and the Courtyard (upper $200 range). Our romantic recommendation here is the Library, with its multiple windows and hardwood floors. The two of you will enjoy the comfortable couch that sits at the foot of a king-sized carved sleigh bed. Both face a fireplace flanked by bookcases. A romantic extra is a separate charming dining room with built-in cupboards, a table, and two upholstered chairs. The Library's bathroom is equipped with a shower and a spa tub for two.

THE FACTS

Eight rooms, each with private bath; some with fireplaces and spa tubs for two. Complimentary full breakfast buffet served in parlor. Wine and refreshments served in afternoon. Handicapped access. Smoking is not permitted. No minimum stay requirement. Moderate to expensive.

GETTING THERE

From Highway 29 in Napa, exit east at First Street and follow signs to downtown Napa. Turn right on California Boulevard and left on Second Street (one way). Follow Second Street to Jefferson Street and turn left. Inn is at the corner of Jefferson and First Streets.

BLACKBIRD INN
1755 First Street
Napa, CA 94559
Telephone: (707) 226-2450;
toll-free: (888) 567-9811
Web site: www.foursisters.com

BLACKBIRD INN

With the 2001 opening of the warm and inviting Blackbird Inn, the Four Sisters Inns group, whose family-run group of romantic properties include nearby Maison Fleurie and Lavender, among many others, have given travelers yet another reason to visit Napa.

The substantial renovation required to convert this fine old Craftsman-style home into an inn with modern luxury amenities might have been more easily accomplished by sacrificing the rich ambience and styling of the original early-twentieth-century structure. Thankfully, the operators preserved and recreated the fine Craftsman detailing, including the liberal use of fine woods that typifies this architectural style.

ROOMS FOR ROMANCE

For traveling romantics, the best value here comes with the rooms featuring spa tubs for two and fireplaces. Among these is room 1 (mid $200 range), which sits at the rear of the first floor, off the main hallway. Guests here are treated to a king-sized four-poster bed and a spa tub for two.

Among our other favorites is room 4 (high $200 range), a rear-facing second-floor hideaway containing all the right elements for a romantic getaway. These include a king-sized iron bed, a corner fireplace, and a spa tub for two. There's also a sleek wall-mounted television and a small private outside seating area. Room 8, a quiet rear-corner room, and the front-facing room 7 are somewhat similarly furnished, equipped, and priced.

Room 6 (mid $200 range) on the second floor is a fairly small corner accommodation whose bathroom has a stall shower.

Blackbird Inn occupies a corner of a bustling intersection that straddles Napa's downtown business and residential districts. The first floor holds a comfortable communal parlor with a massive fireplace. A full breakfast buffet is served here, as are afternoon wine and refreshments.

Outside living areas are confined to the inn's cozy covered front porch. Numerous downtown shops, restaurants, and attractions are within walking distance.

CEDAR GABLES INN
486 Coombs Street
Napa, CA 94559
Telephone: (707) 224-7969;
toll-free: (800) 309-7969
Web site: www.cedargablesinn.com

THE FACTS

Six rooms, each with private bath; four with gas fireplaces and tubs for two. Complimentary breakfast served at tables for two. Complimentary wine and refreshments served in afternoon. No disabled access. Two-night minimum stay required during most weekends. Moderate.

GETTING THERE

From Highway 29 in Napa, exit east at First Street and follow signs to downtown Napa. Turn right on California Boulevard and left on Second Street (one way). Turn right on Jefferson Street and follow for two blocks to Oak Street. Turn left and follow Oak Street six blocks to inn at corner of Oak and Coombs Streets.

CEDAR GABLES INN

The unusual old-English facade of this Napa mansion caught our roving eye during a visit to another grande dame around the corner. Thinking that Cedar Gables Inn might also be worthy of romantic getaway status, we stopped by for a look. Readers will be glad we did.

From the outside, the inn conjures images of Shakespeare's England. But make no mistake; the bard never had it this good. *Romeo and Juliet* might have taken a different turn had Shakespeare spent a night under this roof. Cedar Gables Inn offers some of Napa Valley's most romantic rooms.

ROOMS FOR ROMANCE

We have a number of favorites here. The inn's largest accommodation is named after an aristocratic gent named Count Bonzi, who lived here in the 1920s. Decorated in shades of green, this enchanting room (high $200 range) features a queen-sized carved walnut bed with a soaring headboard. There's also a matching dresser, a gas fireplace, and a sitting area in the windowed corner. The bathroom has a spa tub for two and a shower.

The home's original master bedroom is now called Churchill Chamber (mid to high $200 range). Resplendent in rich, dark woods, the room has a beautiful wall-draped queen-sized bed and a handsome gas fireplace with a mirrored wood surround. The bathroom has a sumptuously draped spa tub for two with a shower.

A new addition is the Gables Suite, which occupies the upper reaches of the mansion. This lofty romantic hideaway features a fireplace, plus a jetted tub placed in a corner of the bedroom near the bed.

Lady Margaret's Room (mid to high $200 range) is somewhat remotely situated and is thus a favorite of honeymooners. Guests here can gaze at the gas fireplace and French-style antiques from the queen-sized bed. The bathroom has a spa tub for two and a separate shower.

A pair of rooms that originally served as servants' bedrooms have been transformed into the Maid's Quarters (mid to high $200 range), a two-room suite. The sitting room is furnished with two soft rocking chairs, while the bedroom contains a queen-sized white iron bed. There's a spa tub for two in the bathroom.

Two other comfortable rooms with queen-sized bed—Edward's Study and Miss Dorothy's Room—were being offered for around $200 at the time of our visit. Miss Dorothy's Room has a gas fireplace and an oversized shower.

Traveling romantics who prefer to breakfast together rather than in typical bed-and-breakfast communal style will appreciate the layout of the Cedar Gables breakfast room, which is thoughtfully furnished with tables for two.

THE FACTS

Ten rooms and suites, each with private bath and deck; some with gas fireplaces and tubs for two. Amenities include TV/DVD players and robes. Complimentary full breakfast served on grounds or in your room. Complimentary wine and cheese served in afternoon. Disabled access. Two-night minimum stay required during weekends; three-night stay required during holiday periods. Disabled access. Expensive to deluxe.

GETTING THERE

From Highway 29 in Napa, take the Trancas exit and turn right. Follow Trancas through Napa. Continue through Silverado Trail light, following sign to Napa/Highway 121, across the Milliken Creek bridge. Turn right at stop sign onto Silverado Trail southbound. Follow for approximately 1 mile to inn's black sign with silver "M," on right.

MILLIKEN CREEK INN
1815 Silverado Trail
Napa, CA 94558
Telephone: (707) 255-1197;
toll-free: (888) 622-5775
Web site: www.millikencreekinn.com

MILLIKEN CREEK INN

A wine-country getaway with a water view? No; you're not suffering from tasting-room overindulgence. That's water—the Napa River to be specific—flowing just outside your picture window.

It's been only recently that Napa has called attention to its namesake river, which flows through town and the adjacent countryside. And while this particular property functioned as an inn under another name for many years, it wasn't until its recent metamorphosis that it caught our eye and beckoned us in for a visit. Today, Milliken Creek Inn ranks easily among the most romantic destinations in the Napa Valley.

With only ten rooms sharing three lush riverfront acres, Milliken Creek is a perfect haven for those who enjoy romancing under the sun and stars as well as under a roof. Rooms are spread among three separate buildings that sit between the Silverado Trail and the Napa River. The river side of the property is an enchanting sweep of towering trees, lawns, sitting areas, gardens, walkways, and fountains, with the lazy, winding river serving as an entrancing backdrop.

ROOMS FOR ROMANCE

The inn is comfortably decorated, and the rooms exude what might best be described as an artful Anglo-Indian-tropical blend. The furnishings are reminiscent of upscale stores like Pottery Barn and Restoration Hardware.

You'll be hard-pressed to discover a more romantic hideaway than room 2 (upper $300 range) in the main building. This expansive corner suite, furnished with a pair of chairs and a separate table and chair set, boasts gorgeous river views and a bed draped in white. A soaking tub sits in an alcove at the rear of the bedroom, while the spacious hardwood-floored bathroom has a separate shower stall. Even the water closet offers a river view.

Equally stunning is room 7 (upper $300 range) in the adjacent South Building, where your private balcony overlooks the river. The two of you will even be treated to a view of the river from bed. There's a cozy corner gas fireplace, and a soaking tub set in an alcove. The bathroom has a tub-and-shower combination. Room 9 is similarly arranged and furnished.

Room 3 (upper $200 range) is a charming tree-shaded hideaway on the second floor, hovering almost directly over the river. The room is quite small, with a bed and only one chair. The bathroom has a tub-and-shower combination.

Although one side of the property faces the Silverado Trail, the innkeepers have done a great job of minimizing traffic noise.

OAK KNOLL INN
2200 East Oak Knoll Avenue
Napa Valley, CA 94558
Telephone: (707) 255-2200
Web site: www.oakknollinn.com

THE FACTS

Four rooms, each with private bath and fireplace. Complimentary full breakfast served at a communal table, tables for two, or in your room. Complimentary early-evening wine and hors d'oeuvres. Swimming pool and spa. No disabled access. Guests staying on a Saturday night must stay three nights total. Four-night minimum stay required during holiday periods. Deluxe.

GETTING THERE

From Highway 29, drive north and turn right on Oak Knoll Avenue traffic light. Follow Oak Knoll Avenue to Big Ranch Road and turn left. Make a quick right turn back onto Oak Knoll and follow to inn on left.

OAK KNOLL INN

Proprietor Barbara Passino obviously had traveling romantics in mind when she created Oak Knoll Inn: a bucolic setting with lovely views, private entrances, spacious guest rooms with love seats and woodburning fireplaces, and—last but not least—few other guests with whom to share the experience.

Situated in the midst of vineyards off the beaten track between the Silverado Trail and Highway 29 just north of Napa, Oak Knoll Inn is a redecorated farmhouse from which spring two single-story guest-room wings. There are only four rooms here, and each is worthy of a special romantic getaway.

ROOMS FOR ROMANCE

With its stone walls and rich Cabernet colors, room 1 is vintage wine country. Opposite the king-sized brass bed is a cozy corner sitting area with a couch and two comfortable chairs.

Room 2 features a handsome king-sized four-poster canopied bed whose fabric matches the window drapes. In room 5, a couch and two chairs flank the fireplace, which is also visible from the brass bed.

The bathrooms are bright and modern, and feature tub-and-shower combinations. All the rooms have outdoor seating areas. Rooms 1 and 6 are the two end units and thus offer maximum privacy. Room rates run from the mid $200 range to the low $300 range during the winter and in the low-to-mid $400 range during the high season.

While every season brings a changing wine-country scene worthy of a visit, the beautiful pool, spa, and yard, along with the magnificent vineyard and mountain views, make Oak Knoll Inn a particularly nice choice for summer getaways. The inn is also known for its sumptuous breakfasts, which just might feature a tidbit or two from the on-site garden.

THE FACTS

Four rooms, each with private bath; one with fireplace.
Complimentary full breakfast served at tables for two or in
your room. Communal spa. No disabled access. Expensive
to deluxe.

GETTING THERE

From Highway 29 in Napa, drive north past Napa and
Yountville. Turn right at inn's driveway a mile-and-a-half
north of Yountville, directly across from Mustards Grill.
Follow drive to inn at top of hill.

CASTLE IN THE CLOUDS
7400 St. Helena Highway
Napa, CA 94558
Telephone: (707) 944-2785
Web site: www.castleintheclouds.com

CASTLE IN THE CLOUDS

We were introduced to Castle in the Clouds by chance while sitting at a window table in the venerable Mustards Grill on Highway 29 north of Napa. During lunch, we spied a handsome Victorian presiding over the valley from a high hill across the road. After our meal, we set out to investigate, discovering an enchanting view property offering a romantic panorama unmatched in the Napa Valley.

Festooned with gingerbread and other ornate trimmings reminiscent of antique Victorians, Castle in the Clouds is actually a contemporary version, thankfully lacking the chopped-up dark and drafty quarters so common among many of its authentic forebears. Inside are bright, good-sized guest rooms and spacious and open public areas. The "parlor" is more like a modern family room, furnished with a comfortable sectional and a large-screen television, as well as a number of tasteful antiques. The long, ornate back bar with a carved grape motif was a grand fireplace in a former life.

Outside are multiple perches from which to savor the breathtaking and varied vista. Oak, palm, and cypress trees and grapevines grace the inn's eight-plus acres, and a hot tub added during an extensive recent renovation also boasts a valley view. Vineyards bearing famous names like Opus One, Silver Oak, and Mondavi glisten in the distance.

ROOMS FOR ROMANCE

The antique theme carries over into the guest rooms, where handsomely carved European beds, towering armoires, original nineteenth-century art, rich fabrics, and Oriental rugs envelope visitors in a warm, inviting romantic environment.

A private outside entrance leads to the aptly named Honeymoon Suite (low $300 range), whose bay window affords a particularly impressive valley view. Inside are an exquisitely carved king-sized bed and matching armoire, two reclining chairs, and a fireplace flanked by windows. The bathroom has a spa tub for one.

Longing for a trip to Europe? A much less expensive and time-consuming alternative is the Cherub Room (high $200 range), which will have the two of you feeling like you've been transported to the countryside of France or Italy. Towering cypresses frame a gorgeous western view that takes in the gardens, valley vineyards, and distant mountains. This large room boasts a carved bed, a mirrored armoire, and a recessed windowed sitting area with a love seat. The bathroom has double sinks.

You'll feel like a king and queen in the regal, Renaissance Revival four-poster king-sized bed that dominates the Valley View Room (mid $200 range). This colorful room is wallpapered and features a hanging tapestry, as well as Oriental rugs. The bathroom has double sinks.

The Tree Top Room (mid $200 range) looks out over an oak-studded hillside and is furnished in rich golden tones. A beautiful armoire with six-foot-tall carved mirror stands alongside a partially canopied nineteenth-century Italian bed. This room offers a private outside entrance and a small deck.

Lavender
2020 Webber Avenue
Yountville, CA 94599
Telephone: (707) 944-1388;
toll-free: (800) 522-4140
Web site: www.foursisters.com

THE FACTS

Eight rooms, each with private bath and fireplace; cottages and one suite have spa tubs for two. Complimentary full breakfast served at tables for two. Complimentary wine and refreshments served in evening. Disabled access. No minimum-stay requirement. Moderate to deluxe.

GETTING THERE

Yountville is approximately 9 miles north of Napa on Highway 29. From Highway 29, take Yountville exit and turn right. Turn left at Washington Street. At fork in road, stay to right on Yount Street. Turn left on Webber Avenue and follow to inn on right.

LAVENDER

With the pull of Napa to the south and the lure of St. Helena and Calistoga to the north, it's easy to skip right past the tiny wine-country town of Yountville. For many years it was just a stop on the way to somewhere else. These days, it's a definite destination, and those who chance to venture off Highway 29 are well rewarded with a growing number of attractions sure to satisfy the most discriminating shoppers, art aficionados, food lovers, and romance seekers.

Vintage 1870, the winery-turned-shopping-complex was among the first on the scene, as was the world-renowned French Laundry. Then came a couple of resort hotels, spas, and newer restaurants like Bistro Jeanty and Livefire. And let's not forget the places to stay.

Among the newcomers is Lavender, a distinctive little enclave designed to evoke images of Provence. Lavender, as well as nearby Maison Fleurie and others in this book, is operated by Four Sisters Inns.

Situated on a corner just a couple of blocks from the main street in a quaint residential area, Lavender is perfectly situated for Yountville explorations. Guests will find that they can leave their cars parked, as the town's shops and restaurants are just a short stroll away.

The inn consists of a vintage home and three very private cottage units, each with two rooms. These face a common lawn and are surrounded by colorful garden areas.

ROOMS FOR ROMANCE

We were fortunate to enjoy a night in one of the cottages, each of which is accessed through its own wooden gate and a small private patio. All the cottages have large spa tubs for two in bathrooms with concrete floors.

Our room, cottage 3 (mid $200 range), is just steps from the main house and is situated behind an ivy-covered fence. The cottage is decorated in a French country motif. A lushly dressed king-sized bed dominates the room and is flanked by two wicker chairs. A delicate vine pattern is stenciled on the walls. A small cabinet conceals a television, and a gas fireplace took the chill off a brisk fall night. The tiled bathroom holds double sinks and a combination deep soaking tub and shower. The other cottages have similar features.

In the main house, room 8 (mid $200 range) is an upstairs suite offering floor-to-ceiling French windows and a bathroom with a spa tub for one. Room 7 (mid $200 range), located on the main level of the house, has a private deck with a two-person hot tub.

Breakfast is served in a rear-facing dining room of the main house. There's also outdoor seating.

THE FACTS

Five rooms, each with private bath, gas fireplace, and spa tub for two. Complimentary full breakfast served at restaurant next door. No disabled access. Two-night minimum stay required during weekends. Moderate.

GETTING THERE

Yountville is approximately 9 miles north of Napa on Highway 29. Take first Yountville exit and turn right. Turn left onto Washington Street and follow for three blocks. At fork in road, follow to right onto Yount Street and to inn on left.

PETIT LOGIS INN

Given the intimate size of Yountville, it's fitting that one of the town's most charming inns consists of only five intimate guest chambers. In fact, Petit Logis translates from the French as "small dwelling."

It's an apt description. Tucked discreetly between the town's main street and a quaint residential neighborhood, this family-operated inn is easy to overlook. It wasn't until we nearly stumbled into it during a walk from another inn to dinner that the inn caught our eye.

From the street, Petit Logis might be mistaken for another quaint Yountville home. But venture up the walkway and you'll see the guest room wing unfold toward the rear of the property, which is adjacent to Yountville's tiny downtown. With Petit Logis as your home base, you're just steps away from such wine-country culinary icons as Bouchon, Bistro Jeanty, and the internationally acclaimed French Laundry.

Also within a short stroll are the Vintage 1870 winery-turned-shopping complex, art galleries, and multiple day spas.

PETIT LOGIS INN
6527 Yount Street
Yountville, CA 94599
Telephone: (707) 944-2332
Web site: www.petitlogis.com

ROOMS FOR ROMANCE

Although the interior decor varies, you can't go wrong with any of the five rooms. Each has a fireplace, chairs, a television, and a refrigerator. The bathrooms each have a spa tub for two and a separate shower.

At the time of our travels, rates at Petit Logis were around $200 for a high-season weekend night. Tariffs are even more reasonable during winter and spring months.

THE FACTS

Thirteen rooms, each with private bath. Complimentary full breakfast served at tables for two. Complimentary wine and refreshments served in afternoon. Spa and swimming pool. Disabled access. No minimum night stay requirement. Moderate to expensive.

GETTING THERE

Yountville is approximately 9 miles north of Napa on Highway 29. Take first Yountville exit, and turn right. Turn left onto Washington Street and follow for three blocks. At fork in road, follow to right onto Yount Street and to inn on left.

MAISON FLEURIE
6529 Yount Street
Yountville, CA 94559
Telephone: (707) 944-2056;
toll-free: (800) 788-0369
Web site: www.foursisters.com

MAISON FLEURIE

If we gave awards for the most enchanting wine-country inns, Maison Fleurie might just walk away with the prize. Located in a charming neighborhood of older homes and across the street from a vineyard, this enticing enclave exudes French-country charm and has loads of curb appeal.

The focal point is a stunning century-old vine-clad brick-and-stone building, which houses the public areas and a handful of guest rooms. A next-door building that in an earlier life served as a bakery now holds four spacious and romantic rooms. A neighboring residence, referred to as Carriage House West, has been converted to a pair of guest rooms. The property, whose owners also operate Lavender, includes a walled courtyard whose centerpiece is a large in-ground communal spa. Behind another wall is a good-sized swimming pool, with chaises for lounging during hot Napa Valley summers. Bicycles are also available to guests.

ROOMS FOR ROMANCE

The seven rooms in the main building (low $100 range to around $200) are nicely decorated and cozy, but are fairly small and basic. We liked the two exposed-brick walls in room 4, an upstairs room with an in-room sink, a queen-sized bed, and a tiny bathroom with a shower stall.

Exposed stone walls are found in the second-floor rooms 2 and 3, which face the front and overlook the vineyard. High under the eaves on the third floor, room 7 is a private hideaway with a king-sized bed, a bay window, and a view of the vineyard. The bathroom is equipped with a tub-and-shower combination.

Our favorite romantic retreats are the four large rooms in the adjacent former bakery building known as La Cachette (high $200 range). These bright and cheery rooms have nice fireplaces and large tiled bathrooms with spa tubs for one. French doors in the two downstairs rooms open onto private patios and the swimming pool courtyard, while the two upstairs rooms have small balconies.

Just a bit smaller than the La Cachette accommodations, room 12 in Carriage House West has a king-sized bed and a corner fireplace. This room is at the rear of the house and faces the pool area.

THE FACTS

Fifty rooms, each with private bath and DVD players; most with fireplaces and tubs for two. Twenty-four-hour room service, movie library, swimming pool/spa, steam sauna, exercise room, and day spa. Restaurant and lounge. Smoking is allowed. Disabled access. Two-night minimum stay required during weekends; three-night minimum required during some holiday periods. Deluxe.

GETTING THERE

Follow Highway 29 north past Napa. Turn right on Route 128 in Rutherford; turn left on Silverado Trail and then make an immediate right on Rutherford Hill Road. Follow up hill to resort.

AUBERGE DU SOLEIL
180 Rutherford Hill Road
Rutherford, CA 94573
Telephone: (707) 963-1211
Web site: www.aubergedusoleil.com

AUBERGE DU SOLEIL

The unpleasant reality is that there are precious few of us who have the means to enjoy frequent or extended visits to Auberge du Soleil. However, it's also a fact that certain occasions in the life of a relationship demand the best. It is for those special celebrations that we heartily recommend a stay at this wine-country paradise. You'll discover there's a reason why Auberge du Soleil consistently ranks on the list of the finest resorts in the world. And the two of you will savor the magical memories of your experience for many years. As managing partner George Goeggel says, "You can stay with us for a short time and find yourselves as a couple again."

Despite its thirty-plus-acre size, Auberge du Soleil maintains a discreet presence on the side of a wooded hill above the Silverado Trail. It's placed just high enough to offer sweeping, unobstructed views of the valley.

The complex consists of several multiroom cottages placed along the hillside. Walkways wind past sculptures and through trees and gardens, connecting the cottages with the main building, the swimming pool, and spa. The Spa du Soleil offers an enticing menu of treatments.

ROOMS FOR ROMANCE

The rooms feature earth-colored tiled floors, and the furnishings reflect a subtle Southwestern/Mexican theme. Brightly colored overstuffed couches invite extended lounging, and the beds are luxuriously draped. Most rooms have fireplaces that can be seen from your bed.

The tiled bathrooms want for nothing. They're nicely lighted and feature double sinks, skylights, robes, great bath products, and huge tubs. Many have spa tubs, and some have large romantic showers with dual heads. Nightly rates here start in the mid $600 range.

During our multiple visits, whether in the winter or summer months, we spent as much time lounging on the lovely private tiled deck as we did indoors. The decks are placed so as to afford views of the valley and the surrounding wooded hills. It's not uncommon to wake to a breathtaking scene of hot-air balloons suspended above the valley.

By the way, if a night here simply isn't within your budget, don't assume the Auberge is completely off limits. The resort's world-class restaurant is open to the public, and the adjacent bar, with its valley-view balcony, is a romantic place to spend an afternoon and celebrate togetherness. It doesn't get any better.

THE FACTS

Eighty-five rooms, suites, and lodges, each with private bath and deck; most have fireplaces. Health spa, gym, two swimming pools, seven tennis courts, nine-hole golf course, and croquet lawn. Restaurants and lounges. Disabled access. Two-night minimum stay required during weekends. Deluxe.

GETTING THERE

From Highway 29 in St. Helena, turn right on Zinfandel Lane and follow to Silverado Trail. At Silverado Trail, turn left; then make an immediate right on Howell Mountain Road; follow to Meadowood Lane and turn left. Follow lane to hotel.

MEADOWOOD NAPA VALLEY
900 Meadowood Lane
St. Helena, CA 94574
Telephone: (707) 963-3646;
toll-free: (800) 458-8080
Web site: www.meadowood.com

MEADOWOOD NAPA VALLEY

Readers of our first Northern California *Weekends for Two* volume know of our fondness for Meadowood. First introduced to this fabulous destination through a business retreat many years ago, we have returned on multiple occasions, the most recent being a particularly getaway-worthy anniversary.

Meadowood is a romantic property in every way, from lodging, to enjoying the outdoors, to food and drink. In fact, if your wine-country getaway is to be focused primarily on wine tasting and winery touring, you might want to consider a hotel or inn that has fewer temptations. With a golf course, seven tennis courts, a croquet lawn, two swimming pools, a spa, a workout room, a lounge, and a restaurant, Meadowood is the ultimate all-in-one destination. Many a couple has been known to remain ensconced here for days.

ROOMS FOR ROMANCE

Although the hotel has grown to more than eighty rooms and suites, you'll wonder where they've placed them all. The accommodations, primarily four-plex "lodges," are tucked discreetly among the trees and hills of this expansive property, which sits above the Silverado Trail.

We spent a memorable night in room 14, one of more than a dozen lodge rooms that border the ninth fairway and the croquet lawn. Perched on a gentle slope, this open-beamed one-bedroom suite has a spacious living room with a couch and a chair. In the bedroom, a king-sized bed sits beneath a motorized skylight. There's a second television here, as well as a fireplace at the bedside. The tiled bathroom has an oval-shaped tub for one. Outside is a small deck with a table and chairs.

The most private options include a group of remote Hillside Terrace Lodges between the golf course and the woods (rooms 90 through 96), and Hideaway Lodges (rooms 52 through 59) set against a wooded hillside at the other end of the property. There are a number of units that are more centrally situated within a few steps of the health spa, pools, and tennis courts.

THE FACTS

Five rooms, each with private bath, gas fireplace, television, and videocassette player. Complimentary continental breakfast delivered to your room. Disabled access. Two-night minimum required during high season weekends. Moderate to deluxe.

GETTING THERE

Calistoga is 24 miles north of Napa. From northbound Highway 29, turn right on Lincoln Avenue. Drive one block to inn on left, at corner of Myrtle and Lincoln.

GARNETT CREEK INN
1139 Lincoln Avenue
Calistoga, CA 94515
Telephone: (707) 942-9797
Web site: www.garnettcreekinn.com

GARNETT CREEK INN

Long before the bed-and-breakfast inns, and even before the mineral springs and mud baths became famous, there was California pioneer and visionary Sam Brannan. It was Brannan who purchased a square mile of land here, who was the first to tap the area's potential, and who supposedly gave the town its name.

Inspired by New York's Saratoga resort, Brannan reportedly had a vision of turning his sleepy Napa Valley community into the "Saratoga of California." One evening, as legend has it, after wining and dining some potential investors, Brannan, feeling the effects of the champagne, rose to speak about his development plans. Unfortunately, he concluded by misstating his intentions to "make this the Calistoga of Sarafornia." The name stuck, and Calistoga was incorporated in 1859.

A decade or so later, local businessman Charles Ayer built a trophy home worthy of his success. He lived there only a few years, however, and over the generations the beautiful structure fell into disrepair.

Rather than watch it fade away, three Calistoga neighbors joined forces to rehabilitate the home and give it new life as Garnett Creek Inn. Today, the pale yellow and white Italianate Victorian, with its wraparound porch, gleams with pride as one of Calistoga's most romantic inns.

ROOMS FOR ROMANCE

Inside are five comfortable guest rooms, each with a private bath, a gas fireplace, a television, and a videocassette player. This grand old manor also offers central air and heating, with controls in each room.

The most romantic room in the house is the two-room Lucinda Suite (around $300), which occupies a generous spot on the main floor of the inn. It has a queen-sized iron "medallion" bed, and a sitting room where two comfortable chairs are placed next to a fireplace above which are built-in bookcases. There's also a bay window overlooking the front gardens. The bathroom has a deep soaking tub and a shower for two.

Also on the first floor is Fair Isle (low to mid $200 range), which has a separate entrance off the front porch. The room has a beamed ceiling with a skylight and a queen-size wicker bed. The bathroom has a shower.

On the second floor, Meadow Way (upper $200 range) has a pretty, queen-sized iron "bird bed" intertwined with vines. Its bay window overlooks the front, and the bathroom is equipped with a shower.

Penrose (low $200 range), a cozy hideaway located on the main floor, features a private deck with a separate entrance. The queen-sized bed is illuminated by a skylight, and there's a shower in the bathroom. Spring Morning (around $200) is a small upstairs room with a double bed.

Garnett Creek Inn guests enjoy the convenient walking access to Calistoga's shops and spas. Some of the town's best restaurants are just steps away.

THE FACTS

Twenty-one rooms and suites, each with private bath; many with fireplaces. Complimentary continental breakfast basket delivered to your room. Disabled access. Two-night minimum stay required during weekends. Expensive to deluxe.

GETTING THERE

Inn is located on east side of Highway 29 (called Foothill Boulevard in Calistoga), one block south of Lincoln Avenue.

CHRISTOPHER'S INN
1010 Foothill Boulevard
Calistoga, CA 94515
Telephone: (707) 942-5755
Web site: www.chrisinn.com

CHRISTOPHER'S INN

A recent flurry of construction has brought new romantic accommodations to this tidy enclave along Foothill Boulevard (Highway 29) that has been hosting valley visitors for many years.

Christopher's is a perfect destination for guests who have their sights set on exploring Calistoga. You'll likely leave the car in the parking lot, as the inn is just one block from the town's bustling main street.

Previous guests who haven't dropped by in awhile probably won't recognize the "new" Christopher's, which has grown to include a conference center and a fresh selection of upscale guest rooms. For romantic getaways, we recommend these.

ROOMS FOR ROMANCE

One of our favorites is room 16, called the Ultimate Suite. Decorated in blue, the room features a partially vaulted ceiling, a pair of love seats, and an extended-length queen-sized four-poster bed. There's also a fireplace next to a seductive glass-enclosed spa tub for two. Eight-foot-tall French doors open to a small patio. In the spring, a pair of cherry trees blossoms above this enchanting space.

Room 11 (high $300 range) is a downstairs suite featuring a fireplace, a settee, and a glass-enclosed sunken spa tub for two. The bedchamber is adjacent to a glass door that opens to a tiny private garden patio with a fountain and a table and chairs.

Room 17 on the second floor is similarly furnished but, like the other second-floor rooms, does not have an outdoor living area. This romantic room does have twelve-foot ceilings, however.

Also on the second floor is stately room 19, where a fireplace sits beside a nineteenth-century Dutch inlaid bed. The spa tub is situated so as to capture a view of the fireplace.

At the time of our visit, two additional luxury rooms (low to mid $400 range) were being created.

In the original part of the inn, we also have a soft spot for room 10 (low $200 range), a hidden retreat that has a tiny private deck with an outdoor fireplace. The room is quite small, but it's long been a favorite among traveling couples. We don't recommend the duplex unit at the rear for romantic getaways.

GRAPE ESCAPES

For a sense of wine-making history, be sure to stroll the auto-free zones at SONOMA's Buena Vista Winery, often cited as California's first winery. The 1860s-era stone-walled press house today serves as the tasting room and gift shop. While in Sonoma, we also recommend visits to Gundlach-Bundschu Winery and Ravenswood.

You'll need a full weekend to cover the scores of boutique wineries in DRY CREEK, RUSSIAN RIVER, and ALEXANDER VALLEYS. In the latter region, be sure to stop at Field Stone, a stone-faced cellar that has been carved out of the earth. You'll need an appointment to visit the romantic French-style Jordan Vineyard estate. It's well worth the extra effort.

In the Russian River Valley, Topolos is a Russian-style winery, while Hop Kiln Winery is indeed a former hop kiln and worth a visit. The Rodney Strong winery was designed by a disciple of Frank Lloyd Wright. Korbel Champagne Cellars offers sparkling wine-making tours as well as garden tours.

The Dry Creek area, north of Healdsburg and west of Highway 101, is home to several wineries including Geyser Peak and Chatêau Souverain.

For more information on Russian River Valley wineries and wine-related events, log on to www.wineroad.com or www.sonomawine.com.

TABLES FOR TWO

For picnic supplies, there's an outpost of Oakville Grocery in downtown HEALDSBURG. There are tables out front as well. A number of wineries have their own delicatessens and picnic areas, including Field Stone, Geyser Peak, and Preston.

For an outstanding dinner in SONOMA, try The Girl and the Fig or Café La Haye. In nearby GLEN ELLEN, we enjoyed a romantic dinner at tiny Saffron.

In HEALDSBURG, the dining choices keep growing. Our respected innkeepers rave about Ravenous, as well as the Dry Creek Kitchen and Bistro Ralph's.

SONOMA COUNTY

Sixty-four rooms and suites, each with private bath, compact disc and DVD players, and dual-line telephone. Complimentary continental breakfast served at on-site restaurant. Complimentary wine and cheese served in evening. Restaurant and lounge. Day spa with fitness facilities. Swimming pool and spa. Disabled access. Two-night minimum stay required during weekends. Deluxe.

GETTING THERE

Sonoma is approximately 45 miles north of San Francisco. Entering Sonoma from south on Highway 12, turn right on MacArthur Street, which is about four blocks south of downtown Sonoma. Inn is located on corner of Highway 12 and MacArthur Street.

MacARTHUR PLACE

Originally a three-hundred-acre country estate that included a manor home and a century-old barn, MacArthur Place has come a long way in the few short years since its transformation into an expansive full-service resort/inn. MacArthur Place now consists of more than sixty fresh country-style rooms. There's also an on-site day spa that offers, among its many services, a couples room for tandem massages.

Situated within an easy drive of Sonoma-area wineries and only four blocks from Sonoma's charming downtown area, the inn provides multiple options for local exploring, should the two of you exhaust all other possibilities.

All the rooms have compact disc and DVD players, and there's a compact disc and DVD library on-site. There are also rental bicycles available for toodling around town. Saddles Steakhouse, which has a martini bar, is housed in what was once the estate's barn, and acclaimed Sonoma restaurants are only a short walk away.

ROOMS FOR ROMANCE

The rooms feature a contemporary, comfortable, casual look, with pine beds, wicker chairs, and plaid and floral fabrics. Artwork by local artists adorns the walls.

About half of the rooms are spread among six cottage units, each with four rooms. The ground-floor rooms are classified as standard (upper $200 range), while the upstairs rooms are deluxe (low to mid $300 range).

MacArthur Place also offers a number of romantic suites (upper $300 range to low $400 range) boasting fireplaces and luxurious bathrooms with hydrotherapy tubs for two and special rain showers with massaging jets. These also have private patios or balconies. Rates are lower during winter and spring months and midweek.

MacArthur Place
29 East MacArthur Street
Sonoma, CA 95476
Telephone: (707) 938-2929;
toll-free: (800) 722-1866
Web site: www.macarthurplace.com

THE FACTS

Nineteen rooms, each with private bath and fireplace; most with private balconies. Complimentary breakfast included. Complimentary refreshments served in afternoon. Communal spa. Call for information about policies concerning minimum night stays. Moderate.

GETTING THERE

Sonoma is approximately 45 miles north of San Francisco. Inn is located two blocks from Sonoma Plaza on Highway 12, which is called Broadway in Sonoma.

INN AT SONOMA

We watched somewhat impatiently as construction on this long-awaited inn progressed slowly during our travels. We had to keep reminding ourselves of what our moms always said: "Good things come to those who wait."

Although the doors hadn't opened by the time we put this volume to rest, we're confident in recommending Inn at Sonoma as a destination with romantic potential. It's managed by the family-run Four Sisters Inns, which has expanded the horizons of traveling romantics with such properties as Green Gables Inn in Pacific Grove, as well as Maison Fleurie and Lavender in Yountville (see Napa Valley section), among many others.

ROOMS FOR ROMANCE

Among the inn's attributes are its newness and its ideal location just steps from the more charming side of downtown Sonoma. Behind the California contemporary facade are nineteen fresh guest rooms designed with today's demanding and discriminating travelers in mind. The rooms all have fireplaces and queen-sized beds, and many have private balconies. Additional niceties include free rental bicycles for use in exploring the town and local wineries. There's also a rooftop spa to help you relax after a day of Sonoma sleuthing.

The inn is just two blocks from the picturesque Sonoma Plaza, around which you'll discover historic sites, as well as great shops and Sonoma's best restaurants.

INN AT SONOMA
630 Broadway
Sonoma, CA 95476
Telephone: (888) 568-9818
Web site: www.foursisters.com

47

THE FACTS

Fifteen rooms and suites, each with private bath; several with tubs for two and fireplaces. Complimentary full breakfast served at tables for two. Swimming pool and spa. Disabled access. Two-night minimum stay required during weekends; two-to-three-night minimum stay required during holiday periods. Expensive to deluxe.

GETTING THERE

From Sonoma, follow Highway 12 north and turn left on Arnold Drive at sign to Glen Ellen. Follow to inn on right prior to reaching business district of Glen Ellen.

GAIGE HOUSE INN
13540 Arnold Drive
Glen Ellen, CA 95442
Telephone: (707) 935-0237;
toll-free: (800) 935-0237
Web site: www.gaigehouseinn.com

GAIGE HOUSE INN

If you aren't on the lookout, it's easy to zip right past this handsome, eclectically styled Victorian inn set discreetly among other homes at the edge of tiny Glen Ellen. But while the Gaige House Inn may not shout "look at me" from the street, it's sure to make a bold and long-lasting impression on those lucky enough to spend a night or two here. You'll be hard-pressed to find more romantic accommodations in this part of the wine country.

Conveniently situated for Sonoma Valley wine-road excursions, Gaige House is also near the ruins of Wolf House, which was to have been the fabulous home of writer Jack London. You might find, however, that wineries and historic explorations will take a back seat once you settle in to your room at the inn.

ROOMS FOR ROMANCE

During our visit, brisk fall weather prevented us from enjoying the wonderful pool and lush back-yard gardens. However, the indoor spaces of Gaige House Inn kept us quite entertained. The rooms, whose tasteful decor represents an artful and rest-ful blend of Asian American influences, are designed for romancing and relaxing. Furnishings might include sumptuously wide chaises, tubs for two, fireplaces, and couches.

Priced in the mid $500 range, the luscious Gaige Suite isn't for the faint of pocketbook. However, you'll be treated to a most memorable experience here. It's no surprise that this second-floor corner, with its 180-degree views, is the first choice among honeymooners. Most impressive is the huge bathroom, which in our opinion ranks as the most romantic bathroom in the Sonoma Valley. The centerpiece is a large tub for two, behind which is a decadent shower for two surrounded by glass and glass tile. Tulip-style sinks are mounted on a stainless steel counter.

Creekside (high $500 range) is another unusu-ally stunning accommodation. This suite features window walls of glass that overlook Calabazas Creek. The amenities here include all you could ever dream of, including a king-sized bed, a couch, a whirlpool tub, a fireplace, a shower for two, and a private patio.

Equally impressive is Woodside (mid $500 range), where eight-foot-tall windows overlook a Zen garden and the creek. There's a Japanese-style soaking tub, a two-person shower, a couch, and a fireplace.

There are three comfortable, nicely furnished rooms priced at around $300 per night. Junior suites (around $400) have fireplaces, private decks, and tubs for two.

Adventurous guests can stroll up the road into Glen Ellen for dinner and exploring. We had a wonderful meal here at the tiny Saffron restaurant.

THE FACTS

*Thirty-six rooms, each with private bath; many with fire-
places and tubs for two. Complimentary full breakfast
served at tables for two in dining room; can be delivered to
your room for an additional charge. Complimentary bottle
of wine provided on arrival. Two swimming pools, spa, and
health spa. Disabled access. Two-night minimum stay
required during weekends and holiday periods. Deluxe.*

GETTING THERE

*From Sonoma, drive north on Highway 12 to inn on left in
Kenwood. From Highway 101 in Santa Rosa, drive south on
Highway 12 (also known as Sonoma Highway) to inn on
right in Kenwood.*

KENWOOD INN

If we had only one night to spend in Sonoma Valley and we had our pick of destinations, Kenwood Inn would be our choice. Sure, there are other places that offer fireplaces, cozy love seats, swimming pools, and spa services. But in terms of romantic ambience, Kenwood Inn has no equal in this part of the wine country.

Step through the gates of this walled compound and you'll feel as though you've been swept away to Tuscany. The inn was created in the style of an Italian *pensione,* with enchanting ivy-covered villas, lush gardens, cloistered and arched walkways, and relaxing pool areas.

During our wine-country explorations, Kenwood Inn underwent yet another makeover and expansion that tripled its size. In addition to twenty-four new rooms and suites, the inn now boasts two new Italian style courtyards and a second swimming pool.

Situated close to a number of wineries including Chateau St. Jean, Kenwood Inn also pampers guests with an on-site day spa offering a tempting menu of massages, facials, and treatments. Many of these services are also available in the privacy of your own room.

ROOMS FOR ROMANCE

Choosing a room here is easy. Pick any one, and you won't be disappointed. We sampled an upstairs retreat in one of the rustic-looking but contemporary-style villas. The bed was placed so as to offer a view of the fireplace, and the furnishings were luxurious. A small private balcony was accessed through French doors, and the bathroom had a tub-and-shower combination. Many of the new rooms have fireplaces and spa tubs for two.

KENWOOD INN
10400 Sonoma Highway
Kenwood, CA 95452
Telephone: (707) 833-1293;
toll-free: (800) 536-9663
Web site: www.kenwoodinn.com

APPLEWOOD INN AND RESTAURANT
13555 Highway 116
Guerneville, CA 95446
Telephone: (707) 869-9093;
toll-free: (800) 555-8509
Web site: www.applewoodinn.com

THE FACTS

Nineteen rooms, each with private bath. Complimentary full breakfast served at tables for two or four. Restaurant and lounge. Swimming pool and spa. Disabled access. Two-night minimum stay required during weekends; three-night minimum stay required during holiday periods. Moderate to deluxe.

GETTING THERE

From Highway 101, 2 miles north of Santa Rosa, take River Road/Guerneville exit and drive west 14 miles to Highway 116. Turn left, cross Russian River, and drive a half-mile to inn on left.

APPLEWOOD INN AND
RESTAURANT

The opening of Applewood in the mid-1980s was greeted with enthusiasm in the Russian River Valley, where romantic overnight accommodations have been in short supply. The hospitality and vision of innkeepers Jim Caron and Darryl Notter clearly struck a chord, judging from the expansion that's occurred here recently.

Initially, the inn consisted of a collection of cozy rooms within the historic Belden House, a 1920s-era manse whose designer is thought to have been famed architect Julia Morgan, the inspiration behind Hearst Castle and the grand Ahwahnee Hotel in Yosemite.

In recent years, Applewood has matured while maintaining a special romantic ambience. Today, the inn includes one of the region's up-and-coming restaurants and a number of exceptional suites. Combine these features with an on-site lounge, a swimming pool, and a spa, and you have all the key elements of a romantic destination resort. It's also located within an easy drive of interesting small premium wine-making operations like Hop Kiln, Iron Horse, Sonoma Cutrer, and Korbel.

ROOMS FOR ROMANCE

Our favorite romantic retreats are the suites (around $300) tucked away in the newer Piccola Casa and Gate House. Contemporary, bright, and richly furnished, the suites have bedside fireplaces, verandas or patios, and either showers or spa tubs for two.

The rooms in the main house, all nicely furnished with antiques as well as contemporary and wicker pieces, start in the mid $100 range. One of these lower-priced rooms has French doors that open to a veranda and a private garden area.

The romance of Applewood carries through to dinner, when couples, including wine-country passersby as well as guests, huddle at candlelit tables in the enchanting, casually elegant, barn-inspired restaurant for a quiet meal. (Plan on spending $100 or more for dinner for two plus wine.) The main room features beamed ceilings, two large river-rock fireplaces, lots of windows, and an outdoor deck.

THE FACTS

Eight cottage rooms and suites, each with private bath; most with woodburning fireplaces and dry saunas. Complimentary full breakfast served at tables for two or in your room. Complimentary coffee and tea delivered separately to your room prior to breakfast. Swimming pool. Restaurant. Disabled access. Two-night minimum stay required during weekends. Expensive.

GETTING THERE

From Highway 101, take River Road/Guerneville exit and drive west on River Road to inn on left.

FARMHOUSE INN AND RESTAURANT
7871 River Road
Forestville, CA 95436
Telephone: (707) 887-330;
toll-free: (800) 464-6642
Web site: www.farmhouseinn.com

FARMHOUSE INN AND RESTAURANT

The forebears of the Farmhouse Inn's current owners were among the Russian River Valley's early pioneers, focusing their efforts on cultivating a variety of crops from hops to grapes. Today, the fourth generation of the Bartolomei family is cultivating the romantic spirit at Farmhouse Inn, a one-of-a-kind retreat tucked into a lush corner of this oft-overlooked wine-making region.

Siblings Catherine and Joe Bartolomei, along with their father, Lee, and stepbrother, Mike Tommervik, combined their collective expertise in hospitality, design, and construction to breathe new life into the Farmhouse, which ranks among our top Sonoma County destinations.

They've also created a charming restaurant in the vintage main house. A focal point of the dining room is an impressive round-the-room mural depicting multigenerations of Bartolomeis at work and play. In the mornings, guests enjoy a full breakfast in an adjacent breakfast room.

At the rear of the property is a lawn area and a swimming pool. Across the driveway from the farmhouse sits a picturesque row of interconnected cottages, whose outward appearance conjures romantic travel images of yesteryear.

ROOMS FOR ROMANCE

We spent a night in room 6 (mid $200), a spacious suite with a large living room furnished with a sofa and a comfortable lounge chair, as well as a fireplace and an armoire that houses a compact disc player and a television (accommodates videotapes only; there's no cable out here in the country). The separate bedroom holds an oversized king-sized sleigh bed. The very large bathroom is a romantic destination in and of itself, offering a spa tub for two combined with a rain shower, as well as an unusual romantic extra: a large dry sauna big enough for two people to stretch out comfortably. All rooms except room 2 have a dry sauna.

Room 7 (mid $200 range), which serves as the bridal suite, is similarly equipped and furnished, including a destination bathroom that has a spa tub for two with a drenching rain shower and a double sauna. It also has a separate living room and bedroom and is decorated in silver, cream, and black brocades and silks.

Room 8 (low $200 range) is a quiet, remote end unit. This room has a king-sized bed, a corner sitting area with two overstuffed chairs, and a fireplace. The bathroom has a sauna big enough for two and a spa tub for one.

At the time of our visit, additional improvements and expansion were planned.

THE FACTS

Five rooms, each with private bath; three with gas fireplace. Complimentary full breakfast served at large communal table. Complimentary refreshments served in afternoon. Swimming pool and hot tub. No disabled access. Two-night minimum stay required during weekends; three-night minimum during holiday periods. Moderate to expensive.

GETTING THERE

Healdsburg is 65 miles north of San Francisco. From Highway 101, take Dry Creek Road exit and turn right at stop sign. Turn left on Grove Street and make an immediate left turn on Chiquita. Turn right on Burgundy. At "T" in road, turn left and follow up hill to inn on right.

VILLA MESSINA
316 Burgundy Road
Healdsburg, CA 95448
Telephone: (707) 433-6655
Web site: www.villamessina.com

VILLA MESSINA

We recommend this enchanting aerie with a single caution: Once you're ensconced in your room, you just might not want to tear yourselves away to enjoy all that Healdsburg and the surrounding wine roads have to offer.

Perched on a hilltop high above the town, this impressive two-story manse presides over a seemingly endless vista of hills, vineyards, forests, and distant mountains. And there are plenty of places from which to drink in the glorious view, including the living areas and breakfast room, with multiple twelve-foot-tall doors that open to vista decks. The unusual swimming pool, which incorporates century-old walls from the Simi Winery reservoir, also offers an impressive panorama. After a day of exploring, many guests spend the waning hours of the day on the deck with a glass of wine, watching the sunset.

ROOMS FOR ROMANCE

The inn's most romantic room is Asti (mid $300 range), with lofty ceilings, a king-sized four-poster bed, a fireplace, a private deck, and views that take in the Russian River and Dry Creek Valleys and Fitch Mountain. The bathroom has both a spa tub for two and a shower for two.

We also like the European-influenced French Room (low $300 range) on the first floor. This room has a king-sized four-poster bed and a fireplace flanked by two windows and chairs. The bathroom holds a spa tub, a bidet, and a shower. Geyser Peak, the Sonoma County geysers, and the Alexander Valley are visible from this room.

In the high $200 range is the Burgundy Room, which holds a queen-sized four-poster bed and a fireplace, and offers wonderful views of the Sonoma County geysers, St. Helena, and the Dry Creek and Alexander Valleys. The bathroom has a spa tub for one and a shower.

At the time of our visit, the less elegant but comfortable Italian Room was being offered for less than $200 a night.

THE FACTS

Fifty-five rooms and suites, each with private bath. Complimentary breakfast delivered to your room. Swimming pool and spa. Day spa. Restaurant and lounge. Disabled access. Two-night minimum stay required during weekends; three-night minimum required during certain holiday periods. Deluxe.

GETTING THERE

Healdsburg is 65 miles north of San Francisco. From Highway 101 in Healdsburg, take Healdsburg Avenue/ Central Healdsburg exit and follow Healdsburg Avenue east to hotel at corner of Healdsburg and Matheson Avenues.

HOTEL HEALDSBURG
25 Matheson Street
Healdsburg, CA 95448
Telephone: (707) 431-0414
Web site: www.hotelhealdsburg.com

HOTEL HEALDSBURG

It might be said that the opening in 2001 of Hotel Healdsburg rounded out the range of romantic getaway options in this idyllic Sonoma County community. It might also be argued that this sleek hotel with its destination restaurant helped to put sleepy Healdsburg on the map of "A" list wine-country destinations.

The fifty-five-room full-service hotel occupies a prominent block-long spot facing Healdsburg's charming town plaza. It has the look and amenities of an upscale big-city boutique hotel, but the surrounding vintage storefronts and the lush plaza across the street soften the property's presence.

ROOMS FOR ROMANCE

The rooms are situated in two impressive-looking side-by-side buildings. A glass-enclosed passageway connects the guest floors.

The hotel's "deluxe" rooms (mid $200 range) are fairly standard in terms of size and amenities. For a romantic getaway, we recommend one of the corner rooms (mid $300 range) or a Junior Suite (low $400 range). There are also spacious one-bedroom suites that carry tariffs of around $700 per night.

The corner rooms are quite large and bright, and most offer nice views of the town plaza across the street. These rooms also have huge six-foot-long soaking tubs. Room 307, for example, has a small entry hallway that opens to a spacious room with two chairs and a desk. Open the shutters for a view of the plaza.

Room 317, a corner-facing suite, is larger still, offering a living area furnished with a couch, an armoire, and a small dining table. The large bedroom has a console table and a television.

The bathrooms are spacious and very contemporary, and are done in cast concrete and tile. The guest rooms all feature high-speed Internet access, phones with voice mail, French press coffeemakers, and laundry and valet services. There's also a wine concierge on-site, as well as a fitness room and a lounge with live evening jazz.

Worthy of special note is Dry Creek Kitchen, located on the ground floor of the hotel. It's run by Charlie Palmer, one of the nation's leading chefs and proprietor of New York City's acclaimed Aureole. Palmer himself is in residence much of the year. The restaurant, which ranks among the Northern California wine country's best, features an open kitchen, a live-fire grill, and outdoor garden dining, weather permitting.

The hotel also has a swimming pool and a well-equipped day spa that offers the standard menu of rejuvenating treatments, as well as a couples suite with a private patio, where the two of you can be pampered together.

Finally, be sure to set aside plenty of time to circumnavigate the plaza and visit the quaint shops, cafes, and wine-tasting rooms.

Duchamp
421 Foss Street
Healdsburg, CA 95448
Telephone: (707) 431-1300
Web site: www.duchamphotel.com

THE FACTS

Ten rooms, each with private bath, gas fireplace, television, and compact disc player. Extended continental breakfast served at large communal table and smaller tables. Swimming pool and spa. Disabled access. Two-night minimum stay required during weekends; three-night minimum during holiday periods. Expensive to deluxe.

GETTING THERE

Healdsburg is 65 miles north of San Francisco. From Highway 101 in Healdsburg, take Healdsburg Avenue/Central Healdsburg exit and drive east. Follow Healdsburg Avenue to fourth traffic light. Turn left on North Street for one-half block. Turn right on Foss street; inn's driveway is on left.

DUCHAMP

Travelers seeking a departure from traditional overnight wine-country experiences should love Duchamp, without a doubt the most unusual destination we discovered during our California wine-road journeys.

   Named after French artist Marcel Duchamp, this unique inn consists of multiple and varied structures ranging from contemporary villas to restored vintage cottages bearing the names and artistic inspiration of artists like Warhol and Man Ray. Wonderful sculptures and gardens adorn the three-acre property, which, despite its convenient proximity to the shops of Healdsburg, is a world unto itself.

ROOMS FOR ROMANCE

We found ourselves most intrigued by the six sleek villas (around $300), which flank a beautiful lap pool and spa. These freestanding gems are unlike any accommodations we've seen, and are described by the proprietors as "garden follies." All are similarly furnished in a minimalist style and feature polished concrete floors, ten-foot-high ceilings, and artist-inspired custom furnishings. Minibars separate the bedrooms from the bathrooms, which feature stainless-steel double sinks and giant tiled walk-in showers big enough for two.

   A little creek separates the villas and pool area from the four "artist cottages," actually rehabilitated former private cottage-sized homes. Some of these face a nondescript light-industrial street. Among our favorites is Man Ray (mid $200 range), a creekside cottage whose artistic centerpiece is a pair of red neon lips over the fireplace. The room has a small corner sitting area with two collectible Italian art chairs dating from the 1950s. The bathroom has a shower for two.

   Man Ray is attached to Picasso (around $300), whose separate living room has a comfortable chaise, a small couch, and a fireplace.

   Another favorite, the Andy Warhol cottage (low $300 range), has four rooms and can accommodate three people. It features a boldly colored separate living room, modern furnishings, a fireplace, and, of course, a Warhol poster. There's a bright corner bedroom and a bathroom with a deep Japanese-style soaking tub for two, as well as a separate shower. This cottage has both a private porch and a patio.

   The other cottage (around $300), named after Spanish painter Joan Miró, sits creekside and has a private deck under the redwoods. There's a relaxing daybed next to the fireplace.

THE FACTS

Twelve rooms, each with private bath; five with gas fire-
places; nine with tubs for two. Complimentary full break-
fast served at tables for four or more. Wine tasting bar.
Disabled access. Two-night minimum stay required during
weekends; three-night minimum during holiday periods.
Moderate to expensive.

GETTING THERE

Healdsburg is 65 miles north of San Francisco. From
Highway 101, take Central Healdsburg/Healdsburg Avenue
exit and drive east. Follow Healdsburg Avenue to Grant
Street. Turn right and follow two blocks to inn on corner
of Grant and Johnson Streets.

GRAPE LEAF INN
539 Johnson Street
Healdsburg, CA 95448
Telephone: (707) 433-8140
Web site: www.grapeleafinn.com

GRAPE LEAF INN

Many seasoned wine-country travelers, including ourselves, have developed a jaded "been there, done that" attitude toward some of the antique Victorian homes-turned-inns that dot California's wine-producing regions. Thus, we admit to having initial misgivings as we drove through the quaint neighborhood on our first visit to Grape Leaf Inn. Any preconceived notions we had were immediately erased, however, on stepping into the inn's lovely new wing.

The recent expansion allowed this grand Queen Anne room to breathe, and made way for new public areas and a number of ultraromantic accommodations that rival the best of Northern California's wine country.

ROOMS FOR ROMANCE

Our favorites are the five lushly appointed rooms that are part of the new addition. One of these, Sangiovese (mid $200 range), is on the main level and is accessible to disabled guests. This beautiful room is dominated by a massive, raised four-poster, mahogany king-sized bed. A fireplace with a marble surround is visible from the bed. The opulent bathroom holds a large combination spa tub/shower, and a sink set in a rosewood dressing table.

Upstairs are found the inn's most romantic hideaways. One of our favorites is Syrah (mid $200 range), where an antique faux-bamboo king-sized bed is set under a sky-lit gable accentuated by double stained-glass windows. A charming reading alcove provides another option for relaxing. There's also a fireplace. In the sumptuous marble bathroom, a Japanese-style soaking tub placed under stained-glass windows and a steam shower for two will compete for your attention. Better yet, how about a steam shower in the morning and a bath later?

Mourvèdre (mid $200 range) is an octagonally shaped, antique-furnished corner turret with high ceilings, a custom mural, and a fireplace. The king-sized bed is set under a sky-lit gable, and the bathroom has a spa tub for two under the gables.

Some of the rooms that are part of the original Victorian structure have smaller bathrooms and bedrooms, but are nonetheless charming and romantic. Popular among honeymooners, Chardonnay (mid $200 range) sits under the eaves on the second floor. The V-shaped ceiling over the bed has skylights that look into the trees and open and close on command. Despite its small size, the bathroom has dual sinks and a big tub for two.

For travelers on a budget, Grape Leaf Inn offers some veritable bargains among its original rooms. Pinot Noir, in the low $100 range, is furnished with a queen-sized bed and has a private bath with a tiled shower and a European-style pedestal sink.

For just a few dollars more you can stay in Sauvignon Blanc, a blue-themed room with a king-sized bed and a stained-glass window. Priced at around $200, Gamay Rose is the home's original master bedroom. It has a king-sized bed, and a bathroom with a spa tub for two.

CAMELLIA INN
211 North Street
Healdsburg, CA 95448
Telephone: (800) 727-8182
Web site: www.camelliainn.com

THE FACTS

Nine rooms, each with private bath; one private bath is detached; four with gas fireplaces and four with tubs for two. Complimentary full breakfast served at communal table or on outdoor patio, weather permitting. Complimentary refreshments served in afternoon. Swimming pool. Partial disabled access. Two-night minimum stay during weekends; three-night minimum during holiday periods. Moderate to expensive.

GETTING THERE

Healdsburg is 65 miles north of San Francisco. From Highway 101, take Central Healdsburg/Healdsburg Avenue exit and drive north. Follow Healdsburg Avenue to North Street. Turn right and follow two-and-a-half blocks to inn on left.

CAMELLIA INN

We discovered Camellia Inn over a decade ago during travels that resulted in the first of eight *Weekends for Two* volumes. Although Healdsburg's inn options have grown in the intervening years, the Camellia continues to tempt travelers with its romantic Victorian magic.

The stately Italianate, built in 1869, occupies a large wooded lot in a quiet Healdsburg neighborhood. At one time during its rich past the property served as a hospital, and an adjacent wing added to care for patients now accommodates wine-country visitors.

The lush property includes profuse gardens with over fifty varieties of camellias, towering mature trees, and a large swimming pool.

ROOMS FOR ROMANCE

Our highest recommendations go to the rooms in the wing adjacent to the main house. The Firelight Room (high $100 range), which faces the front gardens, is a study in Victoriana. The room is furnished with a queen-sized canopied bed, and a love seat set in a bay-windowed seating area. The sink is in the bedroom, and the tiny bathroom holds a large tiled shower.

A massive, half-testered bed from a Scottish castle is the focal point of the Royalty Room (high $100 range). The room, which has a private entrance, also boasts three lovely arched windows, a settee, and an antique armoire. The bathroom has a shower.

Two other romantic options are found on the second floor of a structure that at one time served as a water tower. Tower East (low $200 range) occupies a spacious corner and has a sitting area with two chairs. There's also a wicker love seat and a tiny gas fireplace. A large spa tub dominates the small bathroom.

Tower West (low $200 range) looks out over the trees, patio, and pool area. The furnishings include an in-room sink, a queen-sized four-poster pine bed, a gas fireplace, a love seat, and a chair. The small bathroom holds a spa tub for two. The Tower rooms share a small seating area.

Those who savor their privacy might enjoy a night or two in Tiffany (low $200 range), which sits on the first floor at the rear of the inn, with a private entrance off the parking area. This quiet retreat has a tiny enclosed porch, a corner fireplace, two chairs, a four-poster iron bed, and a full bathroom with a spa tub for two.

For romantic getaways we don't recommend the Demitasse Room, whose private bath is across the hall.

THE FACTS

Five cottage rooms, each with private bath, refrigerator, and gas fireplace. Complimentary full breakfast served. Two-night minimum stay required during weekends; three-night minimum during holiday periods. Moderate.

GETTING THERE

From northbound Highway 101, drive past Healdsburg and exit at Dry Creek Road. Turn right on Dry Creek Road and left at stoplight onto Healdsburg Avenue. Drive 1 mile (across from Simi Winery) and turn right up tree-lined drive to inn.

BELLE DE JOUR INN
16276 Healdsburg Avenue
Healdsburg, CA 95448
Telephone: (707) 431-9777
Web site: www.belledejourinn.com

BELLE DE JOUR INN

One of the attractions of Healdsburg is its range of romantic getaway options. Indeed, our many recommended destinations run the romantic gamut from a boutique hotel and a minimalist compound to quintessential cozy Victorians. And for those who prefer a taste of the rural life, we offer Belle de Jour Inn, a lush enclave of country cottages designed with romance in mind.

ROOMS FOR ROMANCE

The entire second level of a reproduction carriage house comprises the Carriage House suite (around $300), one of Sonoma County's most romantically equipped retreats. Under the vaulted ceiling are a wooden four-poster king-sized bed, a bedside fireplace, a pair of wicker chairs facing a set of view windows, a couch, and a spacious spa tub for two in the room. A separate bathroom holds a shower.

The Terrace Room (mid $200 range) is a bright and cheery cottage with vaulted ceilings and lots of windows. It's furnished with a king-sized bed and two comfortable chairs. At the far end of the room, under a valley-view window, sits a large spa tub in a tiled enclosure. There's also a fireplace and a bathroom with a shower.

Once the humble quarters of the property handyman, the Caretaker's Suite (mid $200 range) has been transformed into a spacious, romantic hideaway with a king-sized canopied bed, a table and chairs, and a wood-stove-style gas fireplace. The modern blue-tiled bathroom has a spa tub for two and shower. This room has a private deck.

Two other cottage units, Atelier and the Morning Hill Room, are offered in the high $100 range. Both are equipped with cozy wood-stove-style gas fireplaces. Morning Hill features a more masculine décor, while the sunny Atelier leans toward the feminine.

All of Belle de Jour's cottages feature compact disc players. The grounds are lush and well maintained, and offer hammocks and benches. The entire complex, inside and out, is nonsmoking. Breakfast is served inside or on the deck of the Italianate Victorian home of innkeepers Tom and Brenda Hearn, who also maintain a vintage touring car. The 1925 Star is available at an extra charge for chauffeured local road trips or winery tours.

GRAPE ESCAPES

Highway 128, the scenic mountain pass that connects the rugged Mendocino coast with northern Sonoma County, is home to about a dozen small and medium-sized wineries. Most of these are NORTH OF PHILO. One of our romantic favorites is Husch, where tastings take place in a tiny weatherbeaten farm building. A two-year search led Frenchman Louis Roederer to these hills, where Roederer Estate now crafts some of the world's best sparkling wines.

Visitors are welcome at bucolic Lazy Creek Vineyards, as long as the gate on Highway 128 is open. Otherwise, you'll need to call ahead for an appointment. Also worth a visit is Handley Cellars, whose tasting room is full of exotic bric-a-brac.

In the HOPLAND AREA, there's McDowell Valley Vineyards as well as Fetzer, whose Bed-and-Breakfast Inn at Valley Oaks is described in this section.

One of California's most unusually located wineries —Pacific Star— is in view of the Pacific Ocean north of Mendocino in FORT BRAGG.

For more information on Mendocino County wineries and wine-related events, log onto www.mendowine.com.

TABLES FOR TWO

The Boonville Hotel is our restaurant pick for HIGHWAY 128. In HOPLAND, on Highway 101, try the Hopland Brewery pub and restaurant at the Mendocino Brewing Company. The quaint Thatcher Inn also has a restaurant. Nearby Fetzer Vineyards operates a deli; Obester, Greenwood Ridge, Handley, and Navarro wineries all have picnic areas.

ON THE COAST, Albion River Inn's restaurant has long been acclaimed for its comprehensive wine list, not to mention the views. In MENDOCINO, favorite dining spots include 955 Ukiah Street Restaurant and the bistro-style Moosse Cafe.

MENDOCINO COUNTY

THE FACTS

Ten rooms, each with private bath. Complimentary continental breakfast served in Sundial Room. Complimentary bottle of wine. Swimming pool. Tasting room and deli. Disabled access. Moderate to expensive.

GETTING THERE

Hopland is approximately two hours by car from San Francisco. From Highway 101, turn east on Highway 175 and drive three-quarters of a mile to inn.

BED-AND-BREAKFAST INN
AT VALLEY OAKS
13601 East Side Road (P.O. Box 611)
Hopland, CA 95449
Telephone: (707) 744-7413;
toll-free: (800) 846-8637, ext. 413
Web site: www.fetzer.com

BED-AND-BREAKFAST INN
AT VALLEY OAKS

Three cheers for the folks at Fetzer Vineyards who recognized the potential for the romantic pairing of wine making and sleepovers. It's a concept whose time has come.

The setting is Valley Oaks Ranch, a hundred-year-old property whose original focus was livestock, poultry, hops, and fruit. Cattle and pears gave way to grapes in the 1960s, when the Fetzer clan started making wine, using Valley Oaks Ranch to explore their concept of food and wine. The Brown-Forman Corporation bought Fetzer in 1992.

Today, the centerpieces of the Fetzer Visitor Center include three delightfully refurbished ranch buildings that host overnight guests. The center also consists of a tasting room, a garden offering seasonal tours, and a deli.

ROOMS FOR ROMANCE

There are six rooms in the redwood-sided, cupola-topped Carriage House. Each has a vineyard view and an overstuffed queen-sized bed. Downstairs rooms have private enclosed patios. A downstairs "junior suite" has a separate bedroom and a fully equipped kitchenette. Upstairs are two suites that have view balconies with small bistro tables and chairs, as well as separate sitting areas and large bathrooms with spa tubs. The private bath entries come in handy, since the swimming pool is nearby.

The Haas House, which served originally as the family home of the pre-Fetzer-era Haas family, offers three rooms (around $200). The Haas Room features a view of Duncan Peak, while the Peck and Foster rooms overlook the Fetzer garden and grounds. These rooms have overstuffed queen-sized beds. There's an extra twin bed in the Peck Room. The Haas House guest rooms share a lovely living room with a fireplace. Three traveling couples could rent the entire Haas House.

Prefer to be by yourselves? The Valley Oaks Cottage, formerly the ranch office, is set on the pathway to the ranch's five-acre organic gardens. It has a separate sitting area and a bathroom with a shower. Mature rosebushes line the walkway to the entrance patio, which has a wicker table and chairs set. The views from here include the lawn of the Haas House, huge valley oaks, and distant Duncan's Peak.

THE FACTS

Five rooms, two in main inn with private baths; two with shared bath; cottage with detached bath. Complimentary full breakfast served at communal table. Complimentary evening refreshments. No disabled access. Two-night minimum stay may be required during weekends and holiday periods. Moderate.

GETTING THERE

Anderson Valley is approximately 115 miles north of San Francisco via Highway 101. From Highway 101 north of Cloverdale, follow Highway 128 west. Inn is approximately 5 miles north of Boonville, on left.

PHILO POTTERY INN
8550 Highway 128 (P.O. Box 166)
Philo, CA 95466
Telephone: (707) 895-3069
Web site: www.philopotteryinn.com

PHILO POTTERY INN

Anderson Valley visitors who welcome the slower pace and charm of this comparatively sleepy wine-making region should likewise appreciate the simplicity and charm of the valley's overnight accommodations.

Among these is Philo Pottery Inn, which has served as a comfy inn for over a century. Built in 1886 to serve as a stagecoach stop on the north coast/valley route, the inn, hewn from native redwood, sits at about the halfway point between Cloverdale and Mendocino.

While Highway 128 serves many travelers on their way to and from the coast, there's plenty to keep wine enthusiasts occupied here in the Anderson Valley. Between Philo and the nearby community of Navarro we counted ten or so small premium wineries worth a visit. Driving time to Mendocino is only about thirty minutes.

ROOMS FOR ROMANCE

Attentively restored, this small inn hosts travelers in simple homespun comfort. It's not a luxury inn. Rooms here are among the least expensive we've seen in Northern California's wine country.

Our two favorite accommodations here are Evaline's Room and Celia's Room, each of which is offered in the low-to-mid $100 range. Evaline's Room is on the first floor and features a queen-sized antique iron bed. The bathroom has a clawfoot tub-and-shower combination, and there's a little private porch with a table and two chairs overlooking the garden.

Also on the first floor, Celia's Room has a queen-sized bed flanked by two windows. There's also an additional twin bed in this room. The private bathroom is equipped with a shower.

The inn also offers a simple, rustic cottage (low $100 range) that's heated by a wood stove. Take note that the private bath is detached.

For romantic getaways, we don't recommend Donna's Room or Lynn's Room, which share a bath.

THE FACTS

Ten cabins, each with private bath, fireplace, and porch. Breakfast, lunch, and dinner are included in daily rate. Dining room, tennis courts, swimming pool, and horseback riding. Children and pets are welcome. No disabled access. Deluxe.

GETTING THERE

Anderson Valley is approximately 115 miles north of San Francisco via Highway 101. From Highway 101 north of Cloverdale, follow Highway 128 west to Philo. Turn left on Philo-Greenwood Road and follow 1 mile to ranch sign. Follow dirt road for 4 miles to ranch.

HIGHLAND RANCH
18941 Philo-Greenwood Road
(P.O. Box 150)
Philo, CA 95466
Telephone: (707) 895-3600
Web site: www.highlandranch.com

HIGHLAND RANCH

Highland Ranch represents a departure from our traditional romantic getaway destinations. By any definition this is a completely self-contained resort. A single set daily rate covers not only your lodging but meals, wine, cocktails, recreation, and even horseback riding. Think of it as a dude ranch for traveling romantics.

Arguably the nicest accommodations in the Anderson Valley, Highland Ranch consists of 250 acres that include meadows, mountains, forests, and a two-acre bass lake. You and your partner, along with your equine companions (more than a dozen horses reside here) have access to hundreds of miles of trails. There are also a swimming pool and two tennis courts, and mountain bikes are available.

Guests are treated to a hearty country breakfast, lunch, and a European-and-American-inspired dinner accompanied with wine or cocktails.

ROOMS FOR ROMANCE

The accommodations are ten comfortable cabins. These have private bathrooms, brick fireplaces, easy chairs or sofas, and porches with rocking chairs. At the time of our visit, the all-inclusive day rate was around $300 per person plus a requisite gratuity.

THE FACTS

Four rooms, two with private baths. Complimentary full breakfast served at communal table or smaller tables. Dinners available at extra cost Thursdays through Sundays. No disabled access. Two-night minimum stay required during holiday periods. Moderate.

GETTING THERE

Inn is on the east side of Highway One 9 miles north of Point Arena and 8 miles south of Elk. Mendocino is about a thirty-minute drive away. Plan on a forty-minute drive from Anderson Valley wineries.

VICTORIAN GARDENS
14409 South Highway One
Manchester, CA 95459
Telephone: (707) 882-3606

VICTORIAN GARDENS

For most, a weekend wine-country getaway to the Anderson Valley means spending the night either in a local bed-and-breakfast inn or in the Mendocino area. Having been tipped to a charming small inn south of Elk, we followed our hearts and set out on winding Greenwood Philo Road heading northwest out of Philo. Less than an hour later, we found ourselves on coastal Highway One at Victorian Gardens.

The inn doesn't advertise, and there's no B&B sign out front, so most passersby probably assume this to be the Victorian home of some lucky locals. Luciano and Pauline Zamboni are indeed lucky locals, but their home is open to traveling romantics in-the-know.

Luciano, a physician and former head of the pathology department at Harbor-UCLA Medical Center, and Pauline, a former city planner and director of capital projects at UCLA, fled the frenetic pace of Southern California a decade or so ago. They bought the ninety-plus-acre Victorian Gardens, enlarged the Victorian house, and fashioned a small inn where great food and a bucolic atmosphere combine to create memorable romantic getaways.

ROOMS FOR ROMANCE

The sprawling Victorian, with its cupola, gables, and graceful front porch, is framed by a traditional white picket fence. Inside are just four guest rooms. They're individually decorated and feature antique lace curtains, beautiful rugs, and original artwork by such masters as Picasso and Warhol. A resident woodworker spent three years restoring and replacing the moldings, banisters, and ceiling trim with native woods.

We recommend the Master Bedroom and Northwest (both in the mid $200 range), which are the two rooms with private bathrooms. The Master Bedroom has a sitting area, a private deck, and armchairs. The bathroom has a shower, a bidet, and a clawfoot tub.

Arguably more romantic, the Northwest room features a bathroom equipped with a tub for two. The bedroom is furnished with a four-poster bed and has a reading area and a rocking chair.

The Golden and Poppy Rooms share a bathroom, but the bath can be your own if you reserve it accordingly.

If you're visiting Wednesday through Sunday, we encourage you to settle in and enjoy the highly acclaimed, authentic multicourse Italian dinners served up by the couple. (Plan on spending in the mid $100 range per couple, including wine and other beverages.) The dining room is also open to travelers spending the night elsewhere.

THE FACTS

Twenty rooms, each with private bath and fireplace; four-teen with oversized or spa tubs; eighteen with private decks. Complimentary full breakfast served in dining room at tables for two. Restaurant and bar. Two-night minimum stay required during weekends; three-night minimum stay during some holiday periods. Disabled access. Expensive to deluxe.

GETTING THERE

Albion is 6 miles south of Mendocino. From intersection of Highways One and 128, drive north on Highway One to inn on left.

ALBION RIVER INN
3790 North Highway 1 (P.O. Box 100)
Albion, CA 95410
Telephone: (707) 937-1919;
toll-free: (800) 479-7944
Web site: www.albionriverinn.com

ALBION RIVER INN

We can't think of a much more romantic weekend than touring a few small premium wineries, enjoying a picnic lunch, lingering over a long, special dinner, and spending a night in an ocean-view room. The Anderson Valley provides the first pair of ingredients; Albion River Inn serves up the last two—in world-class style.

Located just a couple of miles north of the junction of Highways One and 128, and about six miles south of Mendocino village, Albion River Inn has been a personal favorite of ours for years. In addition to its convenient location affording Mendocino exploring as well as Anderson Valley winery touring, the inn offers a setting that's probably the most dramatic of our wine-country destinations. Here a mix of quaint contemporary cottages hug a high, rugged ocean bluff where the Albion River meets the Pacific. With its colorful gardens and boundless vistas, it's a particularly romantic spot.

Wine lovers will enjoy the inn's restaurant, which has an acclaimed wine list, at last count numbering over six hundred different selections. The cellar is sufficiently and appropriately stocked to have earned *Wine Spectator* magazine's Award of Excellence for many consecutive years.

ROOMS FOR ROMANCE

In terms of romantic ambience, we doubt that you'll find a more romantic room anywhere in Northern California than the spa tub equipped ocean-view rooms and cottages here. For example, room 20 (low $300 range) has a king-sized bed, at the foot of which is a cozy seating area with two comfortable wing chairs placed before a fireplace. The bathroom, with its twin vanities, has a spa tub for two placed under a large window that looks out over a rugged ocean cove and the blue Pacific beyond. A similar view awaits on the deck just outside the bathroom door.

Equally impressive is the slightly more masculine ocean-view room 17 (low $300 range), with its dark-tiled fireplace and hearth and dark-stained furniture. This room and its luxuriously equipped bathroom—including a spa tub for two—have similar views.

Romantic rooms with fireplaces, compact disc players, and ocean views, but with more standard bathrooms, are offered in the low $200 range. There are no televisions to spoil the experience. Our guess is that you won't even know they're missing.

THE FACTS

Ten rooms and a vacation cottage, each with private bath; eight with fireplaces and bay/ocean views. Complimentary breakfast served at your door. No disabled access. Two-night minimum stay required during weekends. Moderate to expensive.

GETTING THERE

From Intersection of Highways 128 and One, drive north on Highway One. Inn is a half-mile north of Little River and 2 miles south of Mendocino on east side of highway.

GLENDEVEN INN
8205 North Highway One
Little River, CA 95456
Telephone: (707) 937-0083;
toll-free: (800) 822-4536
Web site: www.glendeven.com

GLENDEVEN INN

For those savvy couples who plan to sleep over at this country estate after a day of Anderson Valley winery hopping, we have one piece of advice: End your wine tasting sufficiently early to allow plenty of time to savor Glendeven. A taste of this inn is more heavenly than any wine you're likely to encounter. Better yet, bring a bottle with you. We can't imagine a better pairing than a fine wine and a room at Glendeven, which in our view is one of Northern California's most romantic destinations.

The eye-catching manor house that is the centerpiece of this glorious two-plus-acre property was built almost a century and a half ago for the pioneering Isaiah Stevens family, who came here from Maine. The Stevenses built their home in the style of a New England farmhouse.

Since becoming an inn several decades ago, Glendeven has grown to include a separate guest building, a fantastic suite, and even a two-bedroom vacation cottage.

ROOMS FOR ROMANCE

Don't be concerned about making a poor choice of rooms. All ten have reading areas, feather beds, and compact disc players. Most have fireplaces, private decks, and ocean vistas. Since our last visit, new owners had redecorated many of the accommodations.

Of the five farmhouse rooms, our favorite is the Eastlin Suite (low $200 range), a very spacious two-room hideaway with a small private garden- and ocean-view deck. The sitting room, located just off the deck, has a couch and a fireplace, while the separate bedroom holds a king-sized bed.

Another two-room suite, Bay View (high $100 range) features a warm color scheme and a comfy sitting room with a handsome hand-crafted wood-and-tile fireplace. The bedroom has a queen-sized bed, and a balcony overlooks the gardens and distant ocean.

Romantics on a budget might want to consider the cozy Garden Room that, at the time of our visit, was being offered in the low to mid $100 range.

Stevenscroft, a charming, remote guest building, has four romantic-getaway-quality rooms. Briar Rose (low $200 range) is on the second floor and boasts vaulted ceilings and French decor. This room has a queen-sized bed and a fireplace, as well as a balcony that affords an impressive coastal view. The bathroom has a shower.

We spent a night in Pinewood (low $200 range), which has a king-sized bed, an ocean-view reading nook, and a private deck.

Arguably the most romantic accommodation at Glendeven is the Carriage House Suite (low to mid $200 range), which provides a perfect haven for couples seeking privacy. This remote hideaway has a large skylit living room with a love seat and a fireplace. In the adjacent bedroom is another gas-stove-style fireplace and a king-sized bed. A private balcony faces the gardens and a vintage water tower.

La Bella Vista is Glendeven's vacation rental house. With two bedrooms, two bathrooms, and a full kitchen, this French country-style ocean-view retreat is perfect for couples traveling together.

THE FACTS

Ten rooms, each with gas fireplace, compact disc player, and television; several with tubs for two. Complimentary full breakfast and refreshments in afternoon. Two-night minimum stay required during weekends (one-night weekend stays may occasionally be available); three- and four-night minimum stay required during some holiday periods. Disabled access. Moderate to expensive.

GETTING THERE

The inn is located on Highway One, just south of Mendocino village. Driving time from San Francisco is approximately three and a half hours via Highways 101 and 128; plan on five hours via Highway One.

BREWERY GULCH INN
9401 Highway One
Mendocino, CA 95460
Telephone: (707) 937-4752;
toll-free: (800) 578-4454
Web site: www.brewerygulchinn.com

BREWERY GULCH INN

In more ways than one, the new Brewery Gulch Inn is an impressive testament to the history of this romantic coastal community. Although it was built in 2001, the inn has deep historic Mendocino roots.

The priceless "first growth" redwood logs from which the inn is fashioned were harvested a century and a half ago. They were among those destined for a local sawmill but they disappeared into the bottom of nearby Big River after rainstorms washed them downstream. Inn builder and proprietor Dr. Arky Ciancutti learned about this buried treasure, personally salvaged a number of the logs, and used the wood to build Brewery Gulch.

The inn's location is also historic, having been the site of Mendocino County's first substantial farm, and later, a dairy and a brewery. Situated on a hill not far from the original farm residence, the inn affords great water views as well as vistas that include protected meadow- and forestland.

The beautiful virgin redwood, which over the years acquired warm red, purple, and even blonde tones, is dramatically incorporated into Brewery Gulch Inn. The comfortable reception area is dominated by beams and paneling, and even the reception desk and wine bar use the wood.

ROOMS FOR ROMANCE

All rooms are furnished with leather club chairs placed before gas fireplaces. Each also has a television and a combination radio and compact disc player. The bedroom and bathroom windows and doors are framed with redwood that has mineralized over the generations. The rooms also underwent extensive soundproofing to minimize any traffic noise.

At the high end, Osprey (high $200 range) is a bright corner room whose private deck offers an ocean view. The bed is king-sized, and the bathroom has a soaking tub for two and a shower.

Manzanita (mid $200 range) is another light-filled corner room with a private ocean-facing deck. There's a queen-sized bed, and a bathroom with a spa tub for two and a shower. In the mid $200 range is Madrone, which is also outfitted with a spa tub for two and an ocean-view deck.

Two rooms, Smuggler's Cove and Lookout (mid $200 range), are located on the third floor and are particularly peaceful. Each is reached via a private short staircase and features a great ocean view. The bathrooms have tub-and-shower combinations.

THE FACTS

Six rooms, each with private bath, television, and video-cassette player; most with gas fireplaces and spa tubs. Complimentary full breakfast served at communal table. Complimentary wine and refreshments served in late afternoon. Two-night minimum stay required during weekends. No disabled access. Moderate to expensive.

GETTING THERE

From northbound Highway One, turn left at Little Lake Drive traffic light. Turn left on Lansing Street and make a quick right onto Little Lake Street. Drive two blocks to inn on right.

C.O. PACKARD HOUSE
45170 Little Lake Street
Mendocino, CA 95460-1065
Telephone: (707) 937-2677;
toll-free: (888) 453-2677
Web site: www.packardhouse.com

Two of our chief goals in producing the *Weekends for Two* series have always been to help travelers sort through the hype and hyperbole and to provide reliable recommendations for special getaways.

This advance groundwork can be especially useful in Northern California's wine regions, where literally hundreds of inns vie for attention. In quaint Mendocino, we happily found a destination that not only lives up to its promises but measures up to our definition of romance. One of the newest arrivals to the village's bed-and-breakfast scene, the c.o. Packard House is a nineteenth-century Carpenter Gothic–style Victorian that opened in the late nineties. Marin County expatriates Maria and Don Levin drew on their skills as interior designers to rehabilitate the aging mansion and introduce the romantic niceties expected by travelers today.

Although the facade of the inn is Victorian, the innkeepers chose to leave that influence at the door. Inside, you'll find a stylishly eclectic mix that ranges from ancient Egyptian artifacts to Japanese prints to a Parisian sleigh bed.

ROOMS FOR ROMANCE

The beauty of the Pacific View Room (low $200 range) is surpassed only by the ocean- and village views. Under a sloping ceiling sits a handsome California king-sized carved pine bed. A gas fireplace sits in an adjacent corner. The elegant bathroom is accessed through a draped arched doorway. Inside are a spa tub for two and a separate shower.

Guests enter the impressive Garden Court Room (around $200) through the luxury bathroom, where a spa tub is set in a tiled and windowed alcove with a view across the garden to a vintage shingled Mendocino water tower. There's also a separate glass shower. This room, which has a peek of the ocean, is furnished with a queen-sized carved and painted bed from France.

Chapman Point (low $200 range) is furnished in such a way that guests can view the ocean from the king-sized wood-and-iron bed through a window set between the eaves. The fireplace can also be seen from the bed. The bathroom has a spa tub and a separate shower.

The centerpiece of the high-ceilinged Village View Room (around $200) is a king-sized draped iron bed. There's a fireplace in the bedroom and a combination spa tub and shower in the bathroom.

GRAPE ESCAPES

Probably the most famous of this region's wineries is Wente, well known for its sparkling wines and site of a popular annual outdoor concert series. But don't overlook some of the lesser-known wine makers. Fenestra Winery is a family affair run out of a weathered century-old winery, where tastes are dispensed in a comfortable, no-frills environment. Retzlaff Vineyards is another charming family-run winery.

Murrieta's Well is a handsome stone winery built near a natural spring where, as legend has it, the notorious Gold Rush–era bandit Joaquin Murrieta watered his horses.

Concannon Vineyard, with its venerable brick facade, is one of California's oldest wineries, established back in 1883.

On the west side of Interstate 680, we recommend stops at Chouinard and Elliston Vineyards. Chouinard operates from an antique redwood barn and occupies a beautiful, mountain setting.

For more information about this region's wineries and wine-related events, visit www.livermorewine.com.

TABLES FOR TWO

Wente Vineyards operates a highly acclaimed restaurant with an outstanding wine list. Stony Ridge Winery, whose specialties are Italian varietal wines, runs a cafe that serves lunches. If you'd like to dine near the vines, most of the wineries in this region have picnic areas.

In PLEASANTON, our innkeepers recommend Haps Original, and Claude and Dominique Bistro. In LIVERMORE, try Lemon Grass for authentic Thai cuisine.

THE LIVERMORE
VALLEY

THE FACTS

Two rooms, each with private bath. Complimentary full breakfast served at communal table or delivered to your room. Complimentary wine and refreshments served in afternoon. No disabled access. No minimum-night stay required. Expensive.

GETTING THERE

From Interstate 580, take Livermore exit onto Vasco Road south. Follow to end (approximately 5 miles). Turn left on Tesla Road and right on Greenville Road.

THE VINEYARD INN AT CRANE RIDGE
5405 Greenville Road
Livermore, CA 94550
Telephone: (925) 455-8085
Web site: www.vineyardinn-craneridge.com

THE VINEYARD INN
AT CRANE RIDGE

Each day, tens of thousands of commuters and tourists zip up, down, and across the bustling Livermore Valley, oblivious to the more than twenty wineries that dot the pretty back roads outside Livermore and Pleasanton.

One of the newest, producing a couple of thousand cases a year, is White Crane Winery, whose proprietors, Nick and Carole Nardolillo, also operate The Vineyard Inn at Crane Ridge, one of the few winery-inn combinations in California.

It's part of a twelve-acre country estate vineyard that commands a sweeping view of the South Livermore Valley wine region. And each of the two guest rooms here takes full advantage of the impressive vista.

ROOMS FOR ROMANCE

The largest of the inn's pair of rooms is the Starlight Suite (low $200 range), a bright corner room dominated by a gorgeous king-sized sleigh bed. The rolling vineyard view through the small arched window above the bed will melt your stress away. There's also an antique-style electric stove. A sliding door opens to a small private balcony overlooking the rose garden and an expanse of vines. The bathroom is furnished with a spa tub-and-shower combination (for one).

In the Vineyard View room (around $200), a picture-perfect view of a vineyard backed by an oak-studded hillside unfolds through a beautifully draped window visible from the four-poster queen-sized bed. Guests here may enjoy a vineyard sunset from their private balcony. There's also an armoire and a raised antique-style electric stove placed near the foot of the bed. An arched doorway leads to the bathroom, which contains a spa tub-and-shower combination (for one). Both rooms have televisions and videocassette players.

THE FACTS

Ten rooms, each with private bath and spa tub and shower. Complimentary full breakfast made to order and served at tables for two or more or delivered to your room. Complimentary refreshments served in afternoon. Day spa. Swimming pool and two spas. Disabled access. Two-night minimum stay required during weekends and holiday periods. Moderate to expensive.

GETTING THERE

From Interstate 580, take Livermore exit onto Vasco Road south. Follow to end (approximately 5 miles). Turn left on Tesla Road and follow for approximately 2 miles. Turn left onto Cross Road and follow to second driveway on left.

PURPLE ORCHID INN
4549 Cross Road
Livermore, CA 94550
Telephone: (925) 606-8855
Web site: www.purpleorchid.com

PURPLE ORCHID INN

At the time of our visit, Purple Orchid Inn had just emerged from an expansion so impressive that proprietor Karen Hughes refers to the property as a bed-and-breakfast resort. We'd have to agree. In our opinion, it's the Livermore Valley's most romantic destination.

Approaching the impressive inn, we had visions of our childhood years spent assembling tiny structures out of Lincoln Logs. In fact, it's said that this is one of the largest residential log dwellings in the world. This new building houses the guest rooms, an art gallery, a conference room, and a dining room. Behind the inn is a patio area with a swimming pool and two spas.

Treatments, including facials and massages, are offered in the on-site spa or in the privacy and comfort of your guest room, and there's a golf cage and a bunker for practicing your chip shot. In addition to the nearby Livermore Valley wineries, there are seven golf courses within an easy distance of the inn.

ROOMS FOR ROMANCE

It's hard to beat the luxurious wood-paneled Vintner's Estate (mid $200 range) for comfort and romantic potential. It has a king-sized bed, a raised fireplace, a bay-windowed eating area, and a bathroom featuring a spa tub for two as well as a separate shower.

Similarly priced and romantically equipped is Double Eagle, which, in addition to a spa tub for two, boasts an extra-large shower for the two of you and a private patio overlooking the pool area. This room has a queen-sized bed and a fireplace.

A nature scene festoons a wall in the Orchid Retreat (mid $200 range). This large room has two queen-sized beds, two comfortable chairs, a large private sunset-view deck, a fireplace, and a spa tub for two.

Uncle Howard's Wilderness Adventure (mid $200 range) is another room well suited to a special romantic getaway. It features a private deck with an outstanding vineyard view, a beautiful king-sized canopied bed, a spa tub for two, a separate shower, and a raised fireplace, as well as a pair of wing chairs.

Purple Orchid Inn also offers well-appointed rooms with single spa tubs in the upper $100 range.

THE FACTS

Three rooms, each with private bath. Complimentary full breakfast served at communal table or delivered to your room. Communal spa. No disabled access. Two-night minimum stay required during weekends and holiday periods. Moderate to expensive.

GETTING THERE

From San Francisco, follow Interstate 580 east to North Livermore exit. Turn right onto North Livermore, which turns into South Livermore. Turn right on Eighth Street and follow to inn at corner of Eighth and G Streets. From the Tracy area, follow Interstate 580 west to the First Street exit. Turn left on First Street and follow to South Livermore. Turn left on South Livermore and follow to Eighth Street. Turn right and follow to inn.

THE QUEEN ANNE COTTAGE ON 8TH

For Livermore Valley–bound travelers who prefer an in-town experience to a stay in the country, we recommend this charming period home and its lovely little cottage. The Queen Anne Cottage on 8th is situated within walking distance of old-town Livermore, and is within a short drive of the area's wineries.

ROOMS FOR ROMANCE

For romantic getaways, we recommend the Pioneer Cottage (low $200 range), which adjoins the house. Built in 1875, this little charmer is decorated in English-country style and furnished with a sumptuous four-poster canopied queen-sized bed. It also has a romantic sitting room with a fireplace, as well as a television and a videocassette player. The cottage also has a full kitchen, and a luxurious bathroom with a spa tub for two and a separate shower.

If another couple has secured the cottage, we recommend the Country Rose room in the main house (around $200), whose centerpiece is an enchanting lace-canopied queen-sized Chinese rattan bed. A Victorian-style settee sits at the foot of the bed. The large bathroom has an oversized spa tub and a separate custom marble shower. Country Rose has its own private entrance and a balcony that overlooks the inn's brick patio and rock-accented spa.

THE QUEEN ANNE COTTAGE ON 8TH
2516 Eighth Street
Livermore, CA 94550
Telephone: (925) 606-7140
Web site: queenanneon8th.com

THE FACTS

Five rooms, each with private bath (one bedroom has a remote private bath) and refrigerator with complimentary beverages. Complimentary full breakfast served at tables for four or delivered to your room. Complimentary wine and refreshments served in afternoon. Communal spa and fitness room. No disabled access. No minimum-night stay requirement. Moderate to expensive.

GETTING THERE

From Interstate 680, take Bernal Avenue exit west. From westbound Bernal Avenue, turn left onto Foothill Road, follow for a quarter mile. Turn right on Longview Drive and follow to inn's driveway on left.

EVERGREEN

Not too many years ago, couples wanting to spend the night as part of a Livermore wine-country getaway had few choices other than some anonymous hotels and motels. However, the growth of the valley's wine industry has brought a welcome handful of more charming places to settle in for a romantic overnight stay.

In Pleasanton, our pick is Evergreen, which is situated nicely for excursions into Livermore Valley, as well as a couple of boutique wineries in the hills along the west side of Interstate 680.

Evergreen is an impressive multilevel, multiangled contemporary-style home of oak and cedar situated in a nice neighborhood adjacent to Augustin Bernal Park and the wild Pleasanton Ridgeland. This woodsy hillside property, located about five minutes by car from downtown Pleasanton, is lush with trees, shrubs, and even a little brook with trickling waterfalls. There's also an outdoor hot tub, which guests share.

ROOMS FOR ROMANCE

There are two special rooms here that are particularly worthy of romantic getaway status. One is Hideaway (around $200). This remotely situated room has a king-sized canopied bed and an oval-shaped spa tub for two. It has a private deck that faces the parking area.

Our favorite room is the Grand View (mid $200 range), a romantic retreat fit for royalty. The bedroom is dominated by a handsome antique king-sized sleigh bed, which overlooks a raised, tiled corner fireplace. The opulent bathroom has his-and-hers sinks and a dramatically placed, tiled spa tub for two set under multiple windows facing the hillside and gardens. There's also a private deck.

Three other smaller rooms are also offered in the mid $100 range. One has a bathroom that is located away from the room.

EVERGREEN
9104 Longview Drive
Pleasanton, CA 94588
Telephone: (925) 426-0901
Web site: www.evergreen-inn.com

GRAPE ESCAPES

CARMEL VALLEY is home to a handful of small premium wineries, and many operate tasting rooms in Carmel Valley Village. After a taste or two, we recommend the two of you make an appointment to visit those wineries whose vintages you particularly enjoyed.

Highway 152, which connects WATSONVILLE with GILROY, is dotted with a number of charming, boutique wineries like Sarah's Vineyard and Kirigin Cellars.

In SANTA CRUZ COUNTY, the family-operated Bargetto Winery has been catering to locals in and around tiny SOQUEL for generations. Farther north near the Santa Cruz Mountains burg of FELTON, quirky Bonny Doon Winery makes some of California's best wines and labels them with some of the wildest and most whimsical art you'll ever see. Hallcrest, David Bruce, and Byington are also worth a stop. For more Santa Cruz Mountains winery information, log on to www.scmwa.com. For MONTEREY COUNTY winery information, visit www.montereywines.org.

TABLES FOR TWO

Those whose wine-country-getaway home base is Santa Cruz County won't find a more romantic spot than the Shadowbrook in CAPITOLA, where a tiny funicular rail car descends a wooded slope to deposit the two of you at this charming creek-view restaurant.

In CARMEL, we recommend Casanova, the Flying Fish Grill, Anton & Michel, and Nico. Fandango and Joe Rhombi's are excellent dinner destinations in PACIFIC GROVE.

THE CENTRAL COAST

THE FACTS

*Ten rooms, each with private bath; most with fireplaces.
Complimentary full breakfast served at a communal table,
in garden (weather permitting), or in your room. No disabled access. Two-night minimum stay required during
weekends; three-night minimum during holidays. Expensive
to deluxe.*

GETTING THERE

*From Pacific Street near Monterey's historic district, drive
east on Martin Street. Inn is marked by a small sign on right.*

OLD MONTEREY INN
500 Martin Street
Monterey, CA 93940
Telephone: (831) 375-8284;
toll-free: (800) 350-2344
Web site: www.oldmontereyinn.com

OLD MONTEREY INN

It's one thing to be Monterey's first bed-and-breakfast inn. It's quite another to retain the title of the best. Despite the opening of many charming hostelries in the years Old Monterey Inn has been in existence, this regal destination still reigns supreme as the standard bearer in terms of hospitality and comfort.

Operated by longtime proprietors Gene and Ann Swett, who raised a large family here, Old Monterey Inn is an attractive Tudor- and Craftsman-style estate home located in a wooded setting in Monterey's historic district. The surrounding gardens, colorful and well tended, provide a romantic setting for breakfast, weather permitting.

ROOMS FOR ROMANCE

From personal experience, we can tell you that the private Garden Cottage (mid $400 range) is a world-class romantic retreat. This enchanting suite has a sitting room, a fireplace, and a separate bedroom with a luxurious king-sized bed. An in-room spa tub for two is set under a skylight for romancing and stargazing.

Bookworms, as well as romantics, will be drawn to the Library (mid $300 range), a Tudor-style hideaway with book-lined walls and a king-sized bed facing a stone fireplace. This nicely windowed room also features a private sun deck.

In the same price range is the cozy Chawton, a room with its own private garden entrance, a fireplace, and a marble-framed spa tub for two. Stoneleigh (mid $300 range) also has a private entry and a spa tub for two, this one surrounded with tumbled marble pebbles.

Decorated with pine furnishings, Dovecote (upper $200 range) features a redwood-beamed ceiling and a corner sitting area with a fireplace.

The least-expensive room (mid $200 range) is Brighstone, whose French-influenced decor includes a chaise longue, an armoire, and an antique iron bed. The windows look through the branches of an ancient oak to the inn's enchanting garden.

THE FACTS

Fourteen rooms, each with private bath. Complimentary breakfast served at communal tables and at tables for two or more. Complimentary wine and refreshments served in evening. Spa. Disabled access. Two-night minimum stay required during weekends; three-night minimum stay during holiday periods and special area events. Moderate to expensive.

GETTING THERE

From Highway One, exit at Route 68 west (Pacific Grove). Follow Route 68 and stay in left lane as it veers left after David Avenue. At Seventeen Mile Drive four-way stop, turn right. Follow for approximately a half mile to inn on right.

THE INN AT 213 SEVENTEEN MILE DRIVE
213 Seventeen Mile Drive
Pacific Grove, CA 93950
Telephone: (831) 642-9514;
toll-free: (800) 526-5666
Web site: www.innat17.com

THE INN AT 213
SEVENTEEN MILE DRIVE

It's not just the rich and famous who can spend a night on world-famous Seventeen Mile Drive. Thanks to the foresight and dedication of innkeepers Tony and Glynis Greening, who rescued this Craftsman-style estate from decay, the rest of us can enjoy a night or two in lovely Pebble Beach.

Perfectly situated as a home base for excursions into the Carmel Valley wine country (as well as to other area attractions, including the Monterey Bay Aquarium and Cannery Row), The Inn at 213 Seventeen Mile Drive offers guests a varied selection of more than a dozen clean and comfortable rooms located in the main house and adjacent cottage units. The parlor room in the main house has wicker furnishings and a fireplace, and outside there's a communal spa.

ROOMS FOR ROMANCE

You'll feel as if you're staying in a redwood chalet if you choose Guillemot (low to mid $200 range), which has a soaring, vaulted redwood ceiling and large windows with window seats. The room features an understated nautical theme and also boasts a fireplace and a sitting area.

Privacy-seekers will enjoy Pelican (around $200), a rose-covered garden cottage that has a king-sized bed, a sitting area, and a fireplace. Another romantic retreat is Blue Heron (mid $200 range), a sunny room with a garden-view balcony, bay views from the windows, and a king-sized brass bed.

In the main house, where all the guest rooms are on the second floor, a favorite among romantics is Avocet (high $100 range), where French doors open to a balcony with garden- and bay views. This room has a queen-sized bed and a corner sitting area with a small table and chairs.

Outstanding bay views can be savored from Turnstone (low $200 range), which is furnished with antiques, Oriental rugs, and a queen-sized four-poster bed. Sanderling (high $100 range) likewise offers great water vistas.

If the two of you are romantics on a budget, don't be scared away by the tony address of the inn. At the time of our visit, The Inn was offering cozy rooms with queen-sized beds in the mid $100 range; quite a comparative bargain in this region.

THE FACTS

Thirteen rooms and one suite, each with private bath and bay/ocean view. Complimentary full breakfast served at communal tables for four or more. Complimentary refreshments served in afternoon. No disabled access. Two-night minimum stay required during weekends; three-night minimum during holiday periods. Moderate to deluxe.

GETTING THERE

From Highway One, take Route 68 exit west to Pacific Grove. Route 68 becomes Forest Avenue. Follow Forest Avenue to Ocean View Boulevard and turn right; follow for two blocks to inn.

SEVEN GABLES INN
555 Ocean View Boulevard
Pacific Grove, CA 93950
Telephone: (831) 372-4341
Web site: www.pginns.com

SEVEN GABLES INN

One of coastal California's most beautiful and oft-photographed homes, Seven Gables Inn is a showstopper in more ways than one. Outside, the creamy yellow multigabled facade has been featured in television commercials, and turns the heads of nearly all who pass by.

Inside the century-old mansion, the gilded public rooms and guest rooms alike have been beautifully restored and furnished with museum-quality antiques. It goes without saying that spending a night here is a special romantic experience. It's no wonder this inn, set just across the street from Monterey Bay, has been one of Northern California's favorite honeymoon destinations for more than twenty years.

ROOMS FOR ROMANCE

The price of the rooms here, which range from the upper $100 range to nearly $400, depends on the room's size and the expanse of the ocean view.

A night in Victoria (high $200 range) will bring a sly smile from even the most discerning traveler. This opulent room, located in the adjacent guest house, features a bay window and boasts a magnificent view of the ocean and bay. The room's stained glass, ornate ceiling treatments, and luxurious draperies are nearly as awe-inspiring as the view.

Travelers who are enchanted by the seven gables can spend a night in one. The largest is the Bellevue Room (around $300), which has four large windows and a beautiful ocean view, as well as a sitting area with a couch illuminated by a stylish chandelier. The tiled bathroom has a tub-and-shower combination.

Another gabled room, aptly named Gable (high $200 range), is a very private retreat set high on the third floor of the main house with windows on four sides and an ocean view from two. The bathroom is equipped with a shower.

The separate 1880s-era Jewell Cottage (high $300 range) features a living room with a gas fireplace and a view that takes in famous Lover's Point. The bedroom faces the garden and is furnished with a queen-sized bed. There's also a breakfast room with a refrigerator and a microwave. The bathroom is equipped with a shower.

The Breakers (around $300) earned national acclaim with a starring role in a VISA credit card commercial. This room features a gable with two comfortable chairs and a view of the crashing surf across the street.

THE FACTS

Ten rooms, each with private marble bath. Complimentary full breakfast served at communal tables for four or more. Complimentary refreshments served in afternoon. Disabled access. Two-night minimum stay required during weekends; three-night minimum during holiday periods. Moderate to deluxe.

GETTING THERE

From Highway One, take Route 68 exit west to Pacific Grove. Route 68 becomes Forest Avenue. Follow Forest Avenue to Ocean View Boulevard and turn right; follow for one block to inn.

GRAND VIEW INN
557 Ocean View Boulevard
Pacific Grove, CA 93950
Telephone: (831) 372-4341
Web site: www.pginns.com

GRAND VIEW INN

While it lacks the Victorian flair of Seven Gables Inn, its more ornate and famous neighbor and sister property, Grand View Inn holds its own as a memorable, romantic ocean-view getaway destination.

This large and impressive home was built in the early twentieth century by local marine biologist and Pacific Grove's first female mayor, Dr. Julia Platt. In the early 1990s, the Flatley family, longtime owners of the Seven Gables property next door, purchased the estate. The two properties share the same stunning location overlooking the crashing surf of Monterey Bay.

ROOMS FOR ROMANCE

High on our list of recommended rooms and high on the third floor is the romantic Rocky Shores room (around $300), with a picture window facing the ocean as well as smaller rows of windows on both sides. The inn's largest accommodation and the only room on the third floor, Rocky Shores has a queen-sized bed and a tub-and-shower-equipped bathroom finished with rich burgundy marble.

The most often-requested room in the inn is Seal Rocks (around $300), where a set of bay windows frame an awesome ocean view. This room has a queen-sized bed and a marble bathroom with a tub-and-shower combination.

Seascape (high $200 range), a high-ceilinged room located on the second floor, features a partially canopied queen-sized bed and a beautifully draped bay window with great views. The white-and-beige marble bathroom is equipped with a shower.

We're also fond of Mariposa (mid $200 range), which has an unusual L shape and offers a stunning ocean view from the partially canopied queen-sized bed. The bathroom has a tub-and-shower combination.

A recent addition is a refurbished two-bedroom Victorian cottage (mid $300 range for one couple) whose living room offers an ocean view. There are gas fireplaces in the living room and master bedroom. The bedrooms open to a private garden with an antique French fountain.

It's worth noting that while many inns seem to be squeezing the guest experience with later check-in and earlier check-out times, the Grand View and Seven Gables Inns begin welcoming guests at 2:30 in the afternoon. Better yet, the inns allow you to savor the splendor of your room until noon.

SAND ROCK FARM
6901 Freedom Boulevard
Aptos, CA 95003
Telephone: (831) 688-8005
Web site: www.sandrockfarm.com

THE FACTS

Five rooms, each with private bath. Complimentary full breakfast served at communal table, at tables for two, or delivered to your room. Communal spa. No disabled access. Two-night minimum stay required during weekends; three-night minimum during holiday periods. Moderate to expensive.

GETTING THERE

From southbound Highway One in Santa Cruz, drive south toward Monterey for approximately 8 miles. Exit on Freedom Boulevard and turn left at stoplight. Follow Freedom Boulevard over freeway for a half mile. Inn is on right, marked by a large yellow mailbox.

SAND ROCK FARM

Back in the 1880s, Dr. August Liliencrantz bought one thousand acres of the original Rancho Aptos land grant and set about building Sand Rock Farm. In addition to thousands of fruit trees, he planted seventy acres of grapevines and built a winery. In 1907, the good doctor shipped more than 100,000 gallons of wine. With Prohibition looming, wine making gave way to cattle ranching. The original redwood barn still stands, and the ruins of the old winery still attract shutterbugs.

The Liliencrantz home, a strikingly handsome, Craftsman-and-Victorian-style manor that has been expanded over the years, is home today of Sand Rock Farm B&B, one of the proud discoveries we made while poking around the back roads of Northern California.

The inn is operated by Lynn Sheehan, who carries the title of "chef and proprietor." She's a graduate of the California Culinary Academy and has worked at such well-known San Francisco restaurants as Stars, Postrio, Mecca, and Vertigo. Lynn also holds wine tastings, seasonal wine-pairing dinners, and cooking classes.

The estate consists of ten wooded acres in a rural valley and mountain setting, less than one mile from Aptos village in beautiful Santa Cruz County. Guests who establish Sand Rock as their home base may set out for the boutique wineries of Hecker Pass out of neighboring Watsonville, or drive an hour or so to Carmel Valley's wineries.

ROOMS FOR ROMANCE

Our love of sun and water naturally drew us to the Morning Glory room (high $100 range), where an antique brass bed shimmers in the morning sun. An oval-shaped spa tub for two is nestled into a tiled window alcove with a view of an ancient oak that arches over the deck. A gas stove warms a cozy sitting area.

Windows on three sides of the Honeycomb Suite (low $200 range) delight guests here with wonderful garden sights and the sound of fountains. A large wood-framed piece of the home's original wallpaper serves as a headboard for the queen-sized sleigh bed. This room also features a gas stove and an in-room spa in a grotto-style enclosure. The bathroom has a dual-head shower.

The spacious Sunporch Suite (around $200) occupies a wing in what was part of the estate's original ranch house. The large bedroom has a king-sized bed flanked by two windows, and the adjacent glass-wrapped sunroom, connected by French doors, has a sitting area with a sofa bed. This room is also conveniently located near the inn's outdoor hot tub.

The great room of the original ranch house now comprises the Hidden Garden Suite (around $200), which features high ceilings, a queen-sized pine sleigh bed, and a spacious windowed seating area with a lush green vista.

Eva's Garden (high $100 range) is a gable-ceilinged corner room with a two-person spa tub, a half-poster queen-sized bed, and a view of the secluded "Eva's garden."

THE FACTS

Thirteen rooms, each with private bath. Complimentary full breakfast buffet taken at tables for two or taken to your room. Complimentary wine and cheese served in afternoon. Disabled access. Two-night minimum stay required during weekends. Moderate to expensive.

GETTING THERE

From Highway One or Highway 17 in Santa Cruz, follow signs to Highway One north/Half Moon Bay. (Highway One is called Mission Street in Santa Cruz.) Follow Mission Street to Laurel Street and turn left. Follow to inn on right.

BABBLING BROOK INN

The increasing popularity of the Napa and Sonoma Valleys and the accompanying crowds that descend on their highways and byways might lead some travelers to conclude that a quiet day on Northern California wine roads is an experience of the past.

While it may come as a surprise to many, the rugged Santa Cruz Mountains, between Saratoga and Santa Cruz, are home to a number of boutique wineries worthy of tasting and touring. In fact, for Bay Area residents we highly recommend a leisurely romantic weekend itinerary starting in the Cupertino/Saratoga area outside of San Jose, winding along scenic Highway 9 through Boulder Creek and Felton, with a side trip to Bonny Doon, and ending in Santa Cruz. Along the way, you'll encounter wineries like David Bruce, Byington, Hallcrest, and Bonny Doon. World-renowned Ridge Vineyards, perched above Cupertino on Montebello Road, offers million-dollar views from Silicon Valley to San Francisco.

At the end of the day, our top choice for a Santa Cruz sleepover is Babbling Brook Inn, a lush and bewitching property with waterfalls, gardens, a waterwheel, trees, gardens, and, of course, the namesake babbling brook.

ROOMS FOR ROMANCE

The Artist's Retreat (mid $200 range) has *romance* written all over it. Inside is a queen-sized feather bed, a brick fireplace in the corner, and a skylit bathroom. Outside is a large deck with a hot tub.

Sisley (high $100 range) has a corner gas fireplace and a windowed sitting area with two chairs. French doors open to a deck with views of the waterfall and brook.

Van Gogh (low $200 range) features an open-beamed ceiling, a spa tub for two, a gas fireplace, and a private garden-view deck. The FMRS Garden room (low $200 range) also has a spa tub for two.

The Toulouse-Lautrec room (low $200 range) is decorated in raspberry and blue tones and features a windowed sitting area, a queen-sized bed, and a garden-view deck. The bathroom has a spa tub for one.

BABBLING BROOK INN
1025 Laurel Street
Santa Cruz, CA 95060
Telephone: (831) 427-2437;
toll-free: (800) 866-1131
Web site: www.cacoastalinns.com

GRAPE ESCAPES

The wine industry of the Gold Country spans both Calaveras and Amador Counties. In Calaveras County, we
suggest heading for the quaint, authentic mining town
of MURPHYS, home to some of our favorite California
wineries. Ironstone Vineyards is a grand contemporary
winery with a beautiful tasting room that sits above man-
made wine caves. The grounds are lush, and concerts are
frequently held here.

Not far away is Stevenot Winery, where highly rated
wines are crafted on a 160-acre estate sprinkled with old
and new buildings. Black Sheep Vintners is another rustic
venue worth a visit.

For more information about Calaveras County wineries,
visit www.calaveraswines.org.

Wine has been an Amador County industry since the
Gold Rush days, and the region's wine-making history is
on display outside of PLYMOUTH at Sobon Estate, a gen-
uine California landmark winery built in 1856. The old
winery is now the site of the Shenandoah Valley Museum.
From Sobon Estate, more than a dozen SHENANDOAH
VALLEY wineries are within a short drive.

For more information about Amador County wineries
and wine-related events, visit www.amadorwine.com.

TABLES FOR TWO

You'll find picnic tables at most of these rural wineries.
Some, like Story Winery and Amador Foothill Winery, both
in PLYMOUTH, boast gorgeous mountain views.

For a memorable dinner in SUTTER CREEK, we recommend Zinfandels and Sutter Creek Palace. In AMADOR
CITY, just outside Sutter Creek, the Imperial Hotel is also
a good romantic dining choice. In JACKSON, our innkeepers recommend Teresa's.

Murphys Grille, Auberge 1899, and the Murphys
Hotel are popular dinner destinations in MURPHYS in
Calaveras County.

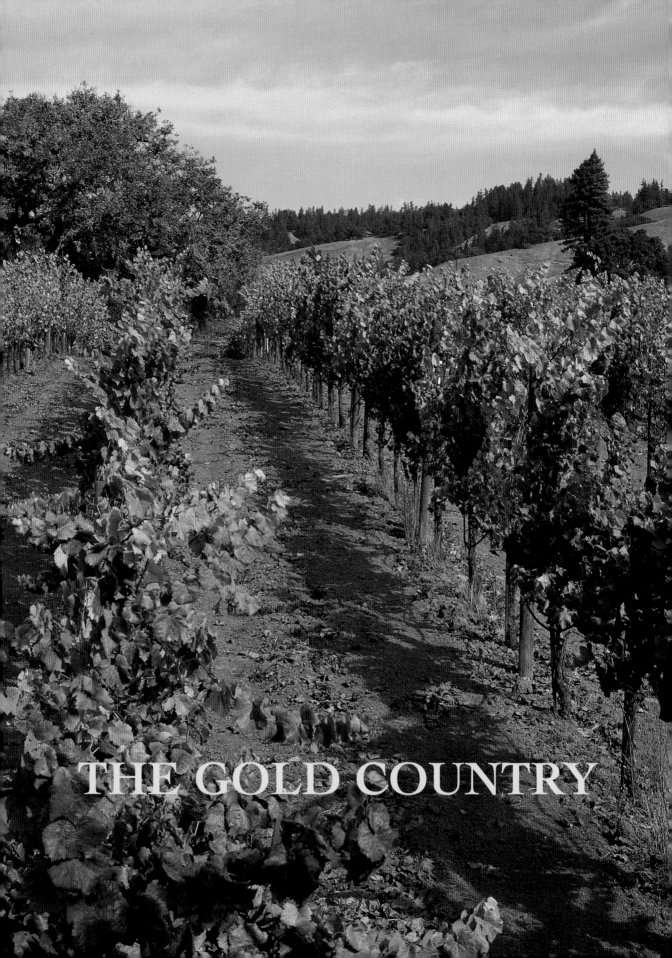

THE GOLD COUNTRY

THE FACTS

Four rooms, each with private bath and electric ambience fireplace. Complimentary full breakfast served at communal table. Swimming pool and hot tub. No disabled access. Two-night minimum stay required at all times. Moderate.

GETTING THERE

Follow either Highway 88 (from Highway 99 near Stockton) or Highway 16 (via Highway 50 from Sacramento) to historic Highway 49. Follow Highway 49 north to Plymouth. Inn is situated just off highway, 3 miles north of Plymouth on right.

INDIAN CREEK BED AND BREAKFAST
21950 Historic Highway 49
Plymouth, CA 95669
Telephone: (209) 245-4648
Web site: www.indiancreek.com

INDIAN CREEK
BED AND BREAKFAST

It's a long way from Hollywood, but Indian Creek Bed and Breakfast traces its romantic roots directly to Tinseltown's early days. The log-walled lodge was created by legendary Hollywood producer and playboy Arthur Hamburger after he finished sowing his wild oats and married Ziegfeld Girl and actress Margaret Breen. The lodge was a wedding gift for the new bride and was used by the couple and their friends as a getaway retreat from the hectic pace of Southern California. It's said that John Wayne was among the many notable guests that slept here.

The lodge's impressive ten acres include scores of oak and pine trees and a spring-fed pond. A long footbridge leads to wild blackberry patches and meadows beyond. Big Indian Creek, which flows through the property, is home to trout and, during summer months, river otters. Wild turkeys, quail, and deer are also in residence.

Guests enter the inn through the impressive Western-themed living and family room where the floors, walls, trusses, and ceiling are crafted entirely of wood and polished logs. The four second-floor guest rooms are set along an open balcony that overlooks the living room.

The inn is very conveniently located for tours of Shenandoah Valley wineries, and guests returning from a day of wine touring are invited to enjoy their bounty at the Cowboy Bar, which once served as a Prohibition-era speakeasy.

ROOMS FOR ROMANCE

Our favorite is the Margaret Breen room (mid $100 range), a front-facing knotty pine paneled hideaway with a king-sized pine bed and wicker chairs. Formerly the lodge's master bedroom, the Margaret Breen also features an electric "ambience fireplace," which resembles a gas log fireplace. It was realistic enough to fool us. Guests who enjoy the outdoors will love the fantastic furnished deck that encircles three sides of this room. It's accessed through French doors. The bathroom has a shower and a pedestal sink.

Horseshoes (positioned so as to hold in the good luck) festoon the queen-sized iron bed in the Western-influenced Way Out West Room (mid $100). This room features a built-in reading nook, an ambience fireplace, and a bathroom with a shower as well as a long (big enough for two), deep bathtub that's original to the inn. A balcony overlooks the pool, spa, and surrounding hills, and stairs lead to a private lower-level deck with lounge chairs.

Dances with Wolves (lower $100 range) is a Native American–themed room with a queen-sized, lodgepole pine bed, an ambience fireplace, and a love seat. The view from this room takes in a wooded hillside, the valley, and creek. The bathroom has a shower stall and a pedestal sink.

THE FACTS

*Ten rooms, each with private bath, compact disc player
and cable television; most with videocassette players.
Complimentary full breakfast served at tables for two or
more or delivered to your room. Rooftop deck. Disabled
access. Two-night minimum stay required during weekends
and holiday periods. Moderate.*

GETTING THERE

*From Highway 99 near Stockton, follow Highway 88 to his-
toric Highway 49. Drive north through Sutter Creek. Inn is
on left at north end of town. From Sacramento via Highway
50, follow Highway 16 east to Highway 49. Drive south on
Highway 49 through Amador City to Sutter Creek. Inn is on
right at north end of town.*

HANFORD HOUSE BED-
AND-BREAKFAST INN
61 Hanford Street (P.O. Box 1450)
Sutter Creek, CA 95685
Telephone: (209) 267-0747;
toll-free: (800) 871-5839
Web site: www.hanfordhouse.com

HANFORD HOUSE BED-AND-BREAKFAST INN

Unlike the region's quintessential B&B inns, which ooze history with all its accompanying creaks and architectural idiosyncrasies, Hanford House is more in tune with today. It's perfect for couples who enjoy spending the day reveling in Gold Country history or wine making but who prefer spending their nights in a more contemporary and luxurious environment.

Housed in a distinctive ivy-covered brick building set among the charming false fronts of this vibrant Gold–Rush era burg, Hanford House is nicely situated for explorations of Sutter Creek and Jackson, as well as the more than twenty wineries of Amador County that are within about a twenty-minute drive. The inn is also within walking distance of Sutter Creek's best restaurants.

ROOMS FOR ROMANCE

The Gold Country Escape Room (low $200 range) is a luxury hideaway on the second floor. A queen-sized canopied feather bed awaits, along with a couch and an ambience fireplace. (We found these units, which combine a heater with the visual image of a flickering fire, at multiple Gold Country destinations.) The bathroom has an oval-shaped spa tub into which two might fit in a pinch. Guests here also have a private rooftop sun deck with a table and chairs.

Among our other rooms of choice is the Roof Top Suite (high $100 range), which is accessed via a separate set of stairs. This romantic room has a queen-sized feather bed and a spacious sitting area with a fireplace. There's also a spa tub for two.

A raised king-sized four-poster cherry bed dominates The Gallery–Arabian Nights room (high $100 range), a high-ceilinged, nicely windowed second-floor chamber. This room also offers a sitting area with a couch and an ambience fireplace.

These three rooms come with complimentary champagne and the breakfast beverage of your choice delivered on silver service.

Another nice room is the Bellisimo, which has a queen-sized four-poster draped bed, a fireplace, and two wing chairs. All rooms have compact disc players; most have televisions.

SUTTER CREEK INN
75 Main Street (P.O. Box 385)
Sutter Creek, CA 95685
Telephone: (209) 267-5606
Web site: www.suttercreekinn.com

THE FACTS

Seventeen rooms, each with private bath; many with fireplaces. Complimentary full breakfast served at communal table. Disabled access. Saturday night stay requires two-night minimum. Moderate.

GETTING THERE

From Highway 99 near Stockton, follow Highway 88 to historic Highway 49. Drive north through Sutter Creek. Inn is on left near center of town. From Sacramento via Highway 50, follow Highway 16 east to Highway 49. Drive south on Highway 49 through Amador City to Sutter Creek. Inn is on right near center of town.

SUTTER CREEK INN

Claiming the title of California's first bed-and-breakfast inn, Sutter Creek Inn is now well into hosting its second generation of romantic travelers. In fact, some of the younger visitors may actually have been conceived on the legendary swinging beds that still hang from the ceilings of this Gold Country gem.

This popular inn, tucked among mature gardens and trees in the heart of downtown Sutter Creek, is a Gold Country landmark. It's even been immortalized on canvas by painter and former Gold Country resident Thomas Kinkade.

ROOMS FOR ROMANCE

While it appears small and modest from the front, Sutter Creek Inn boasts a surprising seventeen rooms with intriguing names like Miner's Cabin, Wood Shed, Upper Wash House, and the Cellar Room.

The Miner's Cabin room (mid $100 range), with its walls of stone, beamed ceiling, and brick fireplace, will give guests a taste of how life may have been in a private home in the mining towns of the Mother Lode. However, the comfy queen-sized bed, the private patio, and private bath with a tub-and-shower combination certainly weren't amenities available to early Sutter Creek settlers.

One of those famous Sutter Creek Inn swinging beds (these can be stabilized for those who might be inclined toward motion sickness) is found in Storage Shed (upper $100 range). This romantic room also has a fireplace, a tub for two, and a separate shower.

Other romantic favorites are the Carriage House (upper $100 range), which features a queen-sized canopied bed and a tub for two; and the Tool Shed (mid $100 range), with a queen-sized swinging bed, a fireplace, a private patio, and a bath with a tub-and-shower combination.

The rooms are spread among the main house and in a smattering of adjacent guest quarters. If bed size is important, take note that some rooms here have double beds.

THE FACTS

Six rooms, each with private bath; one with detached private bath. Complimentary full breakfast served at communal table or delivered to your room. Swimming pool. No disabled access. Two-night minimum stay required during weekends and holiday periods. Moderate to expensive.

GETTING THERE

From intersection of Highway 88 and Highway 49 in Martell, turn north on Highway 49 and then right onto Jackson Gate Road. (If you cross railroad tracks on Highway 49, you've gone too far.) Follow Jackson Gate Road to inn on left. From downtown Jackson, follow North Main Street north from town. North Main becomes Jackson Gate Road. Follow to inn on right.

GATE HOUSE INN
1330 Jackson Gate Road
Jackson, CA 95642
Telephone: (209) 223-3500;
toll-free: (800) 841-1072
Web site: www.gatehouseinn.com

GATE HOUSE INN

For residents of the Bay Area or the inland valley areas, we've got a great alternative to the typical wine-country getaway. Instead of heading to Napa or Sonoma, leave work an hour or two early on Friday and head for the hills of the Gold Country. Highway 88 out of Stockton will whisk you up to the quaint foothill mining town of Jackson in time for a late dinner at one of the town's popular Italian restaurants. And for dessert, well, there's your room at Gate House Inn. That leaves a full day for touring Amador County's wine roads and another sleepover at Gate House.

Located just a stone's throw from town, Gate House Inn enjoys a stunning country setting. The home was once the center of a sprawling estate owned by the pioneering Chichizola family, who supplied Gold Rush miners and ran the old store that still stands in front of the inn.

Although the home has operated as an inn for decades (it changed ownership recently), Gate House retains its period charm, right down to the crackled original varnish on the rich woodwork, and a cast-iron tub that's original to the house. The expansive hillside property, which is surrounded by open tree-studded land, also includes a small orchard, beautiful gardens, a separate rental cottage, a screened game room with a Ping-Pong table, and what surely must have been one of Jackson's first swimming pools.

ROOMS FOR ROMANCE

Our favorite room in the main house is the Woodhaven Suite (mid $100 range), a two-room affair occupying the rear part of the second floor. A wallpapered sitting room has a daybed, bookshelves, and a tiny desk. The spacious bedroom, with its ambience (faux) fireplace, wall of windows, and wood-paneled walls and ceiling, overlooks the rear of the peaceful property. Guests are awakened gently by the rising sun. A clawfoot tub with a rain shower attachment sits behind a door on one side of the room, while the toilet and sink are enclosed on the other side.

Although the second-floor Master Suite is a very nice room, we don't recommend it for romantic getaways as guests have to leave the room to access their bathroom.

Downstairs, the Parlor Room (low $100 range) has a queen-sized bed, nice windows, and a view of the side yard and garden area. The linoleum and tile bathroom contains a shower and the house's original six-foot-long cast-iron clawfoot tub.

We also like the Summer House (mid $100 range), a freestanding cottage with a hundred-year-old grape vine. Formerly the home's summer kitchen, this cozy hideaway has a combination bedroom and sitting room. There's a queen-sized carved bed, a wicker love seat, and a gas stove. You'll step up to the romantic knotty-pine-paneled bathroom with a spa tub for two and a separate shower.

Another great romantic choice is the remote Gate View Cottage (around $200), a self-contained house with two bedrooms, a large living room, a front porch, and a bathroom with a tub-and-shower combination. Outside on a private patio is a large hot tub.

Dunbar House, 1880
271 Jones Street
Murphys, CA 95247
Telephone: (209) 728-2897;
toll-free: (800) 692-6006
Web site: www.dunbarhouse.com

THE FACTS

Five rooms, each with private bath, compact disc player, videocassette player, and refrigerator with complimentary bottle of local wine. Complimentary full breakfast served at communal table, in garden, or delivered to your room. Complimentary refreshments served in afternoon. No disabled access. Two-night minimum stay required during weekends; three-night minimum during holiday periods. Moderate to expensive.

GETTING THERE

From Highway 4 in Angels Camp, drive 8 miles east to Murphys. Turn left on Main Street, then left on Jones, and follow to inn on left. From Murphys Grade Road in Angels Camp, drive 8 miles east to Murphys. Drive through town on Main Street to Jones Street. Turn right on Jones Street and follow to inn on right.

DUNBAR HOUSE, 1880

Although wine making has been under way in California's Mother Lode since the Gold Rush days, the dozen or so small premium wineries of Calaveras County continue to be among the best-kept wine-country secrets in Northern California. Despite its prolific vineyards, interesting wineries, hospitable vintners, rich history, and beautiful surroundings, this region is still waiting to be discovered.

That's good news for romantic travelers yearning for a quiet, unhurried wine-country experience. If you're spending the night (and we highly recommend this), you might want to either begin or end your winery tour with a stop on Main Street at little Milliaire Winery, since it's right across the street from Dunbar House, 1880, Murphys' most romantic inn.

Early California lawmaker Willis Dunbar built this impressive Italianate mansion over a century ago for his new bride, Ellen. The home's romantic history continues in the capable hands of Bob and Barbara Costa, who host discerning travelers in five lovely guest rooms.

ROOMS FOR ROMANCE

On the lower level are Cedar and Sequoia (low $200 range). Cedar, the inn's largest accommodation, consists of Ellen Dunbar's former sewing room and sun porch. It features an outside porch, a queen-sized bed, a spa tub, and a separate shower. Sequoia, formerly the library, has private outdoor seating and a spa tub for two.

Upstairs, the Ponderosa room (around $200) offers a bucolic view of the inn's rose garden. There's a king-sized four-poster bed and a bathroom with a clawfoot tub-and-shower combination.

Also on the second floor is the Sugar Pine Suite (around $200), which has a sitting room, a queen-sized bed, and a private balcony that looks into the trees. In the bathroom you'll find a six-foot-long clawfoot tub and a separate shower.

Nestled high in the attic, Blue Oak (high $100 range) has a queen-sized bed, a private deck, and a clawfoot tub with a hand-held shower.

All rooms at Dunbar House feature high-quality linens from Portugal, televisions, videocassette players (the inn maintains a tape library), compact disc players, reading lamps, makeup mirrors, and hair dryers. You'll even find a complimentary bottle of local wine and appetizers chilling in your in-room refrigerator.

Index

MORE RESOURCES FOR ROMANTIC TRAVELS

WEEKENDS FOR TWO IN NORTHERN CALIFORNIA: 50 ROMANTIC GETAWAYS
The original romantic travel guide that started it all, now in its third edition.

MORE WEEKENDS FOR TWO IN NORTHERN CALIFORNIA: 50 ROMANTIC GETAWAYS
The popular sequel, now in its second edition.

WEEKENDS FOR TWO IN SOUTHERN CALIFORNIA: 50 ROMANTIC GETAWAYS
Intimate destinations from the Santa Barbara coast to the sultry desert, now in its second edition.

WEEKENDS FOR TWO IN THE PACIFIC NORTHWEST: 50 ROMANTIC GETAWAYS
Coastal, mountain, and island hideaways in Oregon, Washington, and British Columbia.

WEEKENDS FOR TWO IN NEW ENGLAND: 50 ROMANTIC GETAWAYS
Places of the heart in Maine, Vermont, New Hampshire, Massachusetts, Connecticut, and Rhode Island.

WEEKENDS FOR TWO IN THE SOUTHWEST: 50 ROMANTIC GETAWAYS
Enchanting destinations in Arizona, New Mexico, and the Four Corners Region.

With more than 150 color photographs and hundreds of room descriptions in each book, these are the definitive travel guides to the nation's most romantic destinations. All are authored by Bill Gleeson and published by Chronicle Books. For additional information about these volumes, visit www.billgleeson.com.

CAST YOUR VOTE! THE WINE COUNTRY'S MOST ROMANTIC HOTEL OR INN

Complete and mail this form to Bill Gleeson, *Weekends for Two*, Chronicle Books, 85 Second Street, Sixth Floor, San Francisco, CA 94105.

Our favorite Wine Country romantic retreat (does not have to be featured in this book):

NAME OF HOTEL/INN: _____

CITY/TOWN: _____

THIS PLACE IS SPECIAL BECAUSE: _____

_____